Complete
Bowhunting

Complete Bowhunting

Hunter's Information Series
North American Hunting Club
Minneapolis, Minnesota

Complete Bowhunting

Copyright© 1987, Glenn Helgeland

Library of Congress Catalog Card Number 87-062919
ISBN 0-914697-08-0

Printed in U.S.A.
1 2 3 4 5 6 7 8 9

Contents

Acknowledgments

Special thanks to NAHC Executive Vice President Mark LaBarbera, Managing Editor Bill Miller and Associate Editor Steve Pennaz for their efforts in planning, editing and laying out this book. Their efforts, combined with those of the author, have put together a guide that will take any hunter from beginner to advanced bowhunter with just a bit of effort on the reader's part. It's a good one.

Thanks also to NAHC Member Products Manager Mike Vail for his coordination and distribution of *Complete Bowhunting*.

Steven F. Burke, President
North American Hunting Club

Photo Credits

All of the photos in this book were provided by the author. Besides relying on his own talents, he called on outdoor photographers Judd Cooney, Dwight Schuh and Pat Miller for the top quality photos in this book.

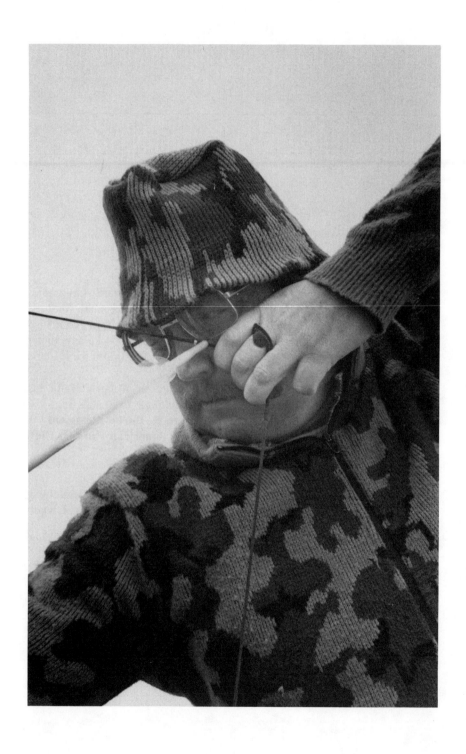

The Author

G lenn Helgeland has been involved in archery and bowhunting
for 20 years. He is now the bowhunting columnist for *North
American Hunter* magazine.

Helgeland edited *Archery World* magazine for 11 years,
1970-1980, and won awards from the National Archery Association for service to archery and from the National Shooting Sports
Foundation for a series of articles, "The Hunter's Story," which
spelled out the contribution sport hunters and hunting have made to
the preservation and strengthening of wildlife populations
throughout North America, and hunters' contributions to conserva-
tion efforts in general and to the general economy.

Helgeland was named, in 1985, as one of the "50 Who Made
A Difference" to the sport of archery/bowhunting over the past 15
years, by the publishers of *Archery World*, *Archery Business*
magazines.

The author has had his archery and bowhunting articles printed
in *Outdoor Life*, *Field & Stream*, *Sports Afield* and other national
and regional outdoor publications.

He is now also is bowhunting columnist for a number of
national and regional archery and outdoor sports publications, and
he has been a member of the *Outdoor Life* bowhunting advisory
panel.

Helgeland is a member and past director of the Outdoor Writers Association of America.

He is now president and co-owner with his wife, Judy, of Target Communications Corporation (TCC) in Mequon, Wisconsin. He has published eight books under his TCC "On Target" banner, and has been a seminar speaker at many bowhunting shows and deer hunting shows throughout the country. He is the producer of four outdoor/hunting shows: Wisconsin Deer Classic, Michigan Deer Spectacular, Red River Hunting/Fishing Expo, and the Tennessee Valley Hunting/Fishing Expo.

Helgeland co-authored with John Williams, 1972 Olympic archery gold medalist, "Understanding Winning Archery," and edited the 2nd edition of the Pope and Young Club's Big Game Records Book. He also was the editor of the book "Archery World's Complete Guide to Bowhunting."

Before becoming involved in archery/bowhunting writing and publishing, Helgeland was an associate editor of *National Wildlife* magazine.

A Wisconsin native, he is a graduate of the University of Wisconsin-Madison in journalism and biology.

The author is a dyed-in-the-wool whitetail deer hunter, but notes that "there's a special attraction in baiting and hunting black bears with the bow. I'm glad I don't need to make a choice between these two aspects of bowhunting; *all* bowhunting is my favorite."

Helgeland has bowhunted whitetails in 15 states and has bowhunted other species in the West and Canada.

He subscribes wholeheartedly to the proven concept that "if you, as a bowhunter, pay the necessary attention to the basics of bowhunting....become a solid bow*hunter*....all the other aspects of bowhunting will fall into line. No matter how good a bowhunter we want to become, nor to what degree we wish to specialize in certain techniques or the hunting of certain species, we cannot afford to ignore the basics. They're the foundation, and without them we cannot be the consistently successful bowhunter we want to be, nor get the fullest enjoyment we wish from this sport."

Dedication

J ust before I wrapped up the last chapter of this book, my family and I skinned and butchered a fat whitetail. We broiled a loin for dinner, seasoning it only with salt and pepper after broiling. Medium rare, it cut easily and tasted sweet and juicy.

I don't recall what else we had with dinner that night, because those items took a back seat to the venison.

So....to the wild game which has gone before it, to that deer, and to that wild game which will fill the future, this book is dedicated. I hope I speak for all of us.

Without the wildlife, there would be no searching, no hunt. With the wildlife, we are richer in life and spirit, at the table, in our memories and, now and then when the Red Gods smile, on our trophy room walls.

Introduction

"Dad, what is bowhunting?"

"Have you got a day to listen? No, of course not. So let me try to summarize it for you."

Dad thought a minute, frowned a couple of times, smiled a couple of times, took a deep breath and .... reached for pencil and paper.

"Just a minute," he said, and scribbled swiftly. Then he handed the paper to the boy.

The youngster examined the words. "But this is just a list," he protested.

"Read it, and remember it as you get more and more involved. With time and experience, you'll understand," Dad said.

The list read:

Bowhunting is:

Time consuming
Time passing swiftly
Great hunting
Details...details...details
Satisfying
Frustrating
Peaceful
Aggressive
Passive
Reflective
Challenging
Biologically educational
Personally rewarding
Quiet
The best way there is
    to spend an autumn day

Violent
Sudden
So near....yet so far
Predatory
Natural
Self-limiting
Self-determining
Addictive
Maddening
Social
Solitary
Family sport
Marriage endangering
Adventurous
An expensive way
  to put meat on the table
Precise
Guesswork
Disappointing
Inspiring
Sophisticated
Simple
Relaxing
Stem-winding
Slow paced
Furious activity

Instantaneous
Long, hard work
Revelatory about the
  wild world and yourself
Big country
Woodlots
Swamps
Ridges
Agricultural crop fields
Edges of cover
Fence rows
Prairies
Mountains
Tundra
Bone-chilling cold
Broiling heat
Homemade
Factory produced
Dedication
Freedom to enjoy
  however you wish
Patience
Individualistic
New and changing
Traditional
A passion
A sport

1

Understanding
Bowhunting & Bowhunters

The reasons we take up bowhunting are immaterial; the fact is, we're here. Nearly all of us came out of the gun hunting legions, simply expanding our hunting opportunities as we became two-season hunters. Some of us remain two-season hunters; others become bowhunters only.

Maybe we became bowhunters because we wanted more of a personal or hunting tool challenge—"There *must* be something more"—or didn't like the crowding we felt with so many other hunters afield during the firearms season, or didn't like the style of hunting as much any more, or the noise or the sometimes-frantic activity inherent to a shorter season.

Maybe we couldn't find a satisfactory place to hunt with a firearm. Maybe we didn't want to have to travel so far to find a satisfactory place.

Maybe we just wanted another excuse to get out in the woods, or wanted more opportunities to *hunt*.

Maybe we just like the grace and silent beauty of the bow and arrow as it is shot. Maybe we are cantankerous individuals, whom no one will hunt with any more.

Maybe we wanted a hunting experience where the family could be more involved; after all, most of us are men, and firearms hunting is traditionally a much more heavily male-oriented activity.

Whatever the reason, bowhunting offers a solution.

I think my situation is fairly typical. My wife likes to bowhunt but has no interest in gun hunting. Our kids have camped with us since they were born. Before that, actually, for my wife hunted mule deer in Colorado when she was four months pregnant with our first child.

On that trip, she also got lost and scared the bejeebers out of me but kept her head and walked downslope until she came to a road. This happened on Labor Day weekend, so the campground she walked into was filled.

The fellow who answered the unexpected knock on his camper door at 10 o'clock that Friday night aged considerably when he peered into the darkness and saw a woman camouflaged from head to toe, carrying a hunting bow, standing there looking up at him. Right then, no doubt, she was a lot more glad to see him than he was her. But he recovered and took her back to base camp.

Our kids will bowhunt when they reach the required age. At least, I think they will; they certainly are showing signs of it. They already are adept at butchering deer and the like.

"This doesn't gross us out like it does other kids in school," is one of their favorite comments, along with "Can we cook some of it right now?"

My son sat in a comfortable oak tree with me this fall and had the nerve to point out a deer to me—describing it in detail—before I even saw it. The little pipsqueak. He laughed when I called him that. Of course, so did I.

Bowhunting is a sport in which it is difficult to be a dilettante. It is a highly individualistic sport, but no matter what our reasons for getting into the sport or the degree of commitment we each have to it, it has ways of whispering seductively into our ear.

Much of this is because of the nature of the sport. If you can get past the misgivings you have the first time you step into the woods with a bow and arrow—"I'm going to kill a deer (or whatever) with this? I must be crazy. I certainly hope no one sees me"—then you can do anything. Your next comment, after some minor but amazing failure where the moment before there was shocking potential for success, is "Aha. There's a possibility."

So you rise to the challenge, intrigued by just how much there may be to learn and just how much potential for success awaits you.

Bowhunting allows parents and children to spend more time together in the field each hunting season.

It will be a humbling experience, but that's alright. It is a leavening experience at the same time, which makes us richer for it all. We didn't exactly go into it with our eyes closed.

The low rate of hunter success means that you can spend a lot of time in search of game before tagging it.

The long seasons keep us from hunting grouse with a shotgun as much as we would like, or keep us off the lakes and streams in the autumn (and during spring turkey and bear seasons) when the fishing is excellent. But these same long seasons also see us camping with friends and/or family when the weather is nice.

Even those who just go along for the campfires and the togetherness enjoy immensely the experience of bow camp. The longer season simply gives us more opportunities to share it in different ways, in different settings, with different people, and in vastly different hunting conditions.

Since we know the challenge and accept it, quite possibly our expectations are a bit lower. Until we get to feeling, "I've got this under control now. Look out, trophies. Here I come."

That is when bowhunting reminds us once again that it is a great sport but very humbling.

But at this stage we sort of like its carrot-and-stick approach, so we collect ourselves and go at it again.

We find that along the way we have become much more knowledgeable about wild animals; in fact, much better woodsmen all around. We are more observant of weather, other wildlife species, food sources for wild animals, terrain, types of cover, the ways animals respond to stress and other stimuli.

We find that we're observing—and enjoying—wildlife at closer distances. We also discover deeper meaning to the word excitement if that wildlife is one we want to put our tag on. We see natural, wild events new to us practically every time we go out. The excitement of discovery is great. It certainly makes interesting conversation later around the campfire.

We find that the bow is, indeed, a limited range hunting tool. Along with this, we humbly discover that even if we are pretty good with it, we still have to know how to *hunt*. Good shooting skill does not automatically equate with hunting skill.

We find that we probably have quite a bit of good bowhunting right close to home, even if we live in the suburbs, and with a little bit of effort we can get permission to hunt it. "Wow! Practically right out my back door!"

Young bowhunters learn from veteran bowhunters. And sometimes, there is even a chance to meet a living legend like Fred Bear.

Our evolution as a bowhunter undoubtedly involves the "human packhorse" stage. That is the time when we near the peak of our "buy-it-and-try-it stage," taking most of that equipment with us to the woods each time, and just before we begin the "serious culling stage." It's amazing how efficient we suddenly become at streamlining, at discovering what is essential and what isn't, at reminding ourselves to "Keep it simple, stupid." But all that experimentation sure was fun, and we wouldn't have learned had we not tried. Nothing ventured, nothing gained.

If you're just beginning, do not begin with trophy-only thoughts in mind. You will be denying yourself great bowhunting experiences, great bowhunting education, great personal satisfaction, and a lot of fine wild game eating, if you stubbornly go the trophy-only route from the beginning. There is great benefit in being able to say "I've been there" when the time *does* come for you to draw down on that big buster.

Remember, too, no matter how deep your experience, that ego problems and "mouth wounds" have caused more problems for bowhunting that anything else. It is easy to believe we hit an animal instead of just barely missing it, especially when the arrow in flight is difficult to follow. That is not a problem until we fail to search for the arrow, or search and don't find it, then open our mouth in careless conversation somewhere and say, "Ah, I hit one but didn't get it."

That is the "Ego Ladder" effect. Bowhunting is such a challenge that sometimes it is tempting to feel that a hit animal is a

At home, in camp or at the local pub, there is always a hunt to remember and a hunt for which to plan

success, whether or not it was recovered. Or that there actually was a hit when there was none at all. The top rung on this ego ladder is a world record trophy; the bottom rung, naturally is, ''I didn't see a thing.'' This ego ladder is a natural thing, but it doesn't need to suffer from abuse. There is a lot to be said for pride in achievement and personal satisfaction.

Nope, bowhunting isn't perfect. Neither are bowhunters. But I *can* tell you that the bowhunting fraternity is an interesting, friendly bunch. (They're all a bunch of liars, of course, when asked where their favorite hunting spots are, but this is understandable. They learned the skill from fishermen.) Once in a while someone will tell you that if you aren't shooting the type of bow and type of arrow he or she is shooting, you aren't a bowhunter. If this happens to you, kindly remind the person that there's plenty of room in this sport for everyone, that no animal yet has been slain by a brand name, and that since this is such an individualistic sport you're going to prove it by doing what suits your fancy. If the person you're responding to is that gung ho about bowhunting, he or she is only attempting to have a lover's quarrel anyway.

Enough of such concerns. Let's go wallow in bows and arrows and bowhunting for a good long while.

2

Get The Right Bow For You

Getting set up with the right archery equipment, especially for the first-timer, can be a confusing process. You may not even know for sure whether you should shoot right-handed or left-handed. You won't know for sure your best draw length or draw weight for the bow to be chosen. You won't know for sure which arrow size is best for your setup. There are different styles of fletching to choose from. Practice arrow points are available in different styles and grain weights. Nocks are available in different styles and sizes.

All this is somewhat like trying to get set up for reloading ammunition without ever having shot firearms.

In The Beginning

The only way to begin is to begin. The ideal beginning is to find a source of top quality advice. If you know an archer or two, check with them for help. Check your local yellow pages for archery or bowhunting clubs, and for archery retailers or sporting goods retailers who have archery/bowhunting gear as one of their product categories.

Dealers will be best set up because they will have a wide range of equipment to examine and a special "try" bow to help check your draw length. They *should* let you try the equipment before you buy it! Obviously, this is most likely to occur at a retail shop which has an archery range. A knowledgeable person helping you will be able to point out how your stance and form should be, where you most likely will be at full draw with a good anchor, etc. This help will do a lot to insure that you get equipment matched properly.

We intend this book to be extremely helpful, but a book cannot provide the "hands on" assistance that a real, live, qualified person can. Additional information sources are listed at the back of this book.

No matter how, where or with whom you begin, remember that each person is physically different, and each shooter has personal preferences. Advice needs to be followed closely, but it shouldn't be followed blindly. You will learn your preferences and equipment matching requirements as you go. With good advice at the outset, you will be able to get properly fitted. This will increase the pleasure and the rewards, and should speed your development. There is no way you can avoid or shortcut this learning process.

"What's The Best?"

Standard question; "What's th*e best*? That's what I want."

There is no "best," because of the individuality of shooting styles, physical makeup, needs and goals. The only "best" equipment is that which you like to shoot, feel confident and comfortable shooting, and which you can afford. For example, the answer to "What's the best broadhead?" is "A razor sharp one."

These answers often frustrate a person, but they are honest and accurate. *You* have to make the decisions; they cannot be made for you. Sure, you can get solid guidance toward making the best decision, but it all comes down to *you*.

The two most important tips are these: 1) *Be sure you and your shooting equipment, bow and arrows, are matched to each other;* 2) *If you want to economize, do so in your bow purchase, not your arrow purchase*. The most expensive bow in the world cannot shoot mismatched and/or crooked arrows. But any bow outfitted with high quality, consistently constructed (shaft to shaft) arrows can produce good groups if those arrows are matched to you and the bow.

Matched Equipment. Matched equipment simply means that if you will be shooting, for instance, a 60-pound peak draw weight bow, and your draw length is 30 inches, you will need arrows of the proper stiffness so they will fly right when those 60 pounds of energy are delivered to the arrow when the bowstring is released.

An arrow that is too short won't permit you to reach full draw and will have a different stiffness than an arrow of proper length; an arrow that is too long will add unnecessary weight and will also be of different stiffness than an arrow of proper length. An arrow which is of proper length but of improper stiffness will also fly poorly or terribly, depending upon how mismatched it is. Poor quality arrows which are inconsistent in stiffness, shaft to shaft, will also cause untold problems.

Remember, too, that *the bow is a short-range hunting tool*. Any arrow shot at 200 feet per second, or faster, is a fast arrow — but its speed is much closer to the speed of a thrown rock than to the slowest bullet. This should be a sobering thought, and all the more reason to understand why you must become an accurate shot *and* a good hunter to be consistently successful with a bow and arrow.

Industry Standards

The Archery Manufacturers Organization (AMO) developed over the years a set of standardized terminology and standardized lengths for bows and bowstrings. This ensures that everyone talks the same language, so when you ask for a 43-inch bowstring you will get a 43-inch bowstring, for instance, and that it will fit all bows marked as 43 inches.

Bows

Under AMO standards, bow draw weights are marked on the bow handle or limb, almost always the limb, for the number of pounds of energy needed to draw the bow to 28 inches. It will say, for instance: 65# @ 28″, or whatever the draw weight is supposed to be for that bow with those limbs.

Always check the draw weight on a scale. Labels can be wrong. If you assume the label is correct when it is not, you will have a headache when trying to get your arrows to fly right because they will not be matched properly.

For the sake of simplification, let's say there are two basic styles of bows: Those without wheels and those with wheels. Bows without wheels are recurves or longbows.

Bows with wheels of some sort are compound, cam or dyna-bow. Compounds have round wheels at limb tips; cam compounds have egg-shaped wheels at limb tips, and dyna-bows have two crescent-shaped units at the tip of the lower limb and no wheel at the tip of the upper limb.

Recurves. Today's working recurve bows are composites of

wood and fiberglass. They may be one-piece or take-down design (usually three pieces, of one handle and two limbs which are bolted or locked in some manner to the handle). They have a centershot design, meaning that a sight window is cut into the handle. This centershot most likely will be deeper on a metal-handle bow than a wood-handle bow because the metal has more homogeneity of construction and more inherent strength.

Solid fiberglass bows are made, but ruggedness is their chief characteristic. Youth camps like them; bowhunters don't.

Recurve bow lengths, measured from limb tip to limb tip at the strung position, range from the mid 40s to 72 inches. Most hunting recurve bows are 50 to 64 inches in length. The shorter the bow length, the less comfortable it is to shoot because the bowstring pinches your fingers at full draw and the less efficient and smooth-drawing it is. Longer lengths are more comfortable, generally, because of the smoother draw, less finger pinch and better balance in your hand (a short stick is easier to move off center than a longer stick). Longer length bows usually store more energy and will shoot a faster arrow. The shorter lengths look more wicked and are easier to carry in brush, but most bowhunters shoot recurves of 58 to 64 inches in length.

A takedown recurve is the easiest bow of all to pack because of its collapsible feature. Recurves in general can be easiest to transport because of their lightness and lack of bulk. Even though a travelling bowhunter may use a compound as his number one bow, chances are he has a disassembled recurve in his pack as insurance.

Many bowhunters who began with recurves and switched to compounds are switching back to recurves. Reasons are mixed, but the lightness and simplicity are factors. The challenge of using a bow that's just a bit tougher to shoot is also a factor. Quietness, easy setup, and ease in moving through brush are all factors.

Most who switch back to the recurve have nothing against the compound. They're just different bows, and the fact that the wheeled bow might give better performance was of less significance than other factors deciding how the bowhunter wished to hunt.

Many standard commercial bow manufacturers have put recurves back in their line. Custom recurve manufacturers have sprung up throughout the country, too, particularly as the pendulum swings back a bit toward a middle ground.

Longbows. The longbow is the bow of Robin Hood and

This is not the time to decide if you've chosen the right bow. You should have complete confidence in your equipment before you set foot in the field.

Howard Hill. It can be a composite of wood and fiberglass, (or wood and sinew) with the fiberglass or sinew only a single surface layer. It does not have the energy storage capabilities of recurve or compound bows and is harsher to shoot, jarring your hand upon release. Those who use it are more interested in the styling and tradition than in maximum mechanical efficiency.

Compound Bows. The principle of the compound bow was developed in the late 1930's, but nothing was done with it until the mid 1960's when Allen Archery began commercial production. The bow's popularity boomed in the early 1970's, and today there are bowhunters who doubt whether game animals can be taken with anything other than a compound bow. Of course, there also are bowhunters who believe you must shoot 70 pounds of draw weight or more to take anything. Sort of makes you wonder.

A young guy stopped to talk with me at a sport show in Boston a couple of years ago and, after polite discussion, asked whether it was, indeed, possible to take a deer with "one of those double-ended bows."

"You mean a recurve?" I asked.

"Yeah, that's it." He smiled at the recognition of the name.

I told him it was, but I don't think he believed me. He is the other end of the spectrum from the traditionalists; if it doesn't have wheels, it isn't a bow.

The compound bow simply uses a system of wheels and cables to gain a mechanical advantage. The *bow reaches peak draw weight in mid draw, then relaxes in draw weight until full draw is reached.*

Early compounds had two limb-tip eccentrically mounted pulleys and two center-mounted pulleys positioned mid-limb. These four-wheelers relaxed in draw weight from 15 to 30 percent at full draw.

The next generation, so to speak, did away with the mid-limb pulleys. These two-wheelers commonly relaxed from 40 to 50 percent of their peak draw weight at full draw. Most of today's compound bows are this two-wheel style.

This design does several things. Since it relaxes in draw weight at full draw, the archer can hold and aim a 60-pound compound more easily than a 60-pound recurve. If the compound relaxes 50 percent at full draw, you're holding only 30 pounds instead of 60 pounds at full draw.

Purists will say you don't get as clean a release with the lower weight on the bowstring, and they will be right, but no one cares much because the difference is insignificant. The increased ability to hold the bow under control at full draw and aim it well and confidently far outweighs the fact that you might have a less than perfect release.

The reduced tension simply means the bow is easier to aim and shoot well and is more fun to shoot.

As a friend says, "If I wanted to get red in the face, shake like a leaf and anchor for no more than a milli-second, I'd go back to my recurve. But I don't, so I haven't."

This reduced tension at full draw also means that you probably will have a longer draw length when shooting a compound than when shooting a recurve. A one-inch increase is the norm.

The rallying cry for compounds was not, however, the ease in shooting. The big thing was the compound could store more energy in its limbs at full draw and thus shoot a faster arrow. It also, theoretically at least, could shoot a much lighter arrow and thus pick up even more speed.

Since there are good compounds and not-quite-so-good compounds, just like there are good recurves and not-quite-so-good recurves, all-inclusive statements like that can be misleading.

A compound *should* store more energy at full draw than a recurve because of a difference in its force-draw curve. There simply is more total resistance encountered during the total length of the drawing of the compound, even if there is less weight at full draw, compared to the recurve. Assuming equal or increased efficiency between the compound and the recurve, the result then should be an ability of the compound to shoot the same arrow faster.

Early proponents of the compound took that one long step further and said that since the arrow shot from a compound is not hit with the peak poundage upon release, but rather after it has started its forward motion, a lighter, less stiff arrow ought to be able to fly right because it won't have to absorb that big wallop right at the start when it is motionless. And that lighter arrows then ought to allow all sorts of arrow speed increases in feet per second. Some of the early ads were almost ludicrous in their efforts to make the customer think he had something approaching a rifle.

The efforts fell off the cliff when most everyone realized they were trying to make Chevy sedans perform like Ferraris.

Too-thin, too-light arrows were outfitted with too-small fletches attached straight down the shaft (for ultimate speed, but minimum stabilization or drag). The results usually were a lot of clattering and clinking as the arrows tried to clear all the cables and sight windows and such, followed by some of the fastest missed shots in the history of mankind!

The setup simply begged for trouble because too-light arrows are extremely tricky to shoot well consistently. That kind of setup is not for most of us; it is, in fact, for very few of us.

The big deal was that anyone who had a compound just knew his bow shot 200 feet per second or more. Didn't matter what the draw weight was, draw length, arrow weight, bow efficiency, etc. Since it was a compound it shot 200 + feet per second—world without end, amen.

I attended an outdoor shoot one autumn at which archers were invited to shoot three arrows through a chronograph and get an average reading of their setup's arrow speed. To make the shooting easier, a deer target was placed 12 yards beyond. The shooter aimed at the deer and his shot went through the chronograph.

One fellow, obviously proud of his bow, plunked three arrows into the deer's cardboard heart but stalked away in disgust when the chronograph showed that his compound shot his arrows only 167 feet per second. His bubble had been burst. It didn't make any difference to him that he put all three arrows in a spot the size of a dime. His compound didn't shoot 200 fps, so nothing else counted.

Actually, an average compound will shoot only 8-10percent faster than an average recurve of equal peak draw weight. Any percentage above that generally is illusory, simply because the recurve shooter either draws to a shorter draw length than he thinks he draws (and thus stores less energy in the limbs), or releases the bowstring before he reaches full draw and a solid anchor (which also stores less energy in the limbs). Since he can draw the compound over the hump, over the mid-draw peak weight, and then hold it comfortably at full draw, *all* the compound's energy is stored. The result is an unfair comparison between the two mechanical devices because of human operator error and gullibility.

Today we have come full circle, for the most part. We shoot arrows matched for peak draw weight at our draw length—just as we did when matching arrows to recurves—and get consistently better clearance and arrow flight. The heavier, stiffer arrow is more forgiving.

We also have gone away from the miniscule fletching, back to larger fletches attached with enough spiral to spin stabilize the arrow as quickly as possible after it leaves the bow.

A few archers still put all their marbles in the ''speed'' basket, reserving none for the ''weight'' basket, but the balance is better today than it once was.

Compounds are available in adjustable and non-adjustable draw weight styles. The forms are usually available in 15-pound increments of adjustability, such as 45-60 pounds or 65-70 pounds. This is an excellent feature, for it permits the adjusting of draw weight to the arrow during tuning. This is a lot more economical than getting new arrows if the first ones you bought don't turn out to be matched as well as you would like.

In addition, you can set the bow at minimum draw weight while you're learning, then move up to a heavier draw weight if desired when you develop your shooting form and muscles. That is more economical than buying a new bow.

Compounds generally are available in incremental draw lengths of two inches, such as 26-28, 28-30, 30-32 inches. This is part of the matching process when you buy a bow. If the bow is not set for your draw length, you still will be able to draw it, but full draw may be reached on the bow before or after you reach your proper draw length. Either way, the bow will not perform as well as it would if shot from the bottom of the valley (distance in inches at which maximum let off is reached). The bottom of this valley should correspond with your draw length for the best, most consistent shooting performance—your's and the bow's.

Dyna-bows. The dyna-bow looks like a bit of a hybrid without a wheel on the upper limb. Two crescents on the lower limb tip work as eccentrics to achieve the letoff at full draw. A nice feature of the dyna-bow is its bottom-heaviness. This gives it balance and stability in your bow hand. This style of bow has its fans, too, but there aren't too many of them.

Cam Bows. The cam bow could be considered to be a generation above the round-wheel compound. This bow features egg-shaped eccentric wheels.

Cam bows often are more pre-stressed than round-wheel compounds, meaning the limbs are under more tension when in the undrawn state. This factor plus the efficiency of the egg-shaped eccentric can make the cam bow a highly efficient, fast bow. However, early designs had to be modified back some because they were a bit too stressed and were too noisy and harsh to shoot. Reducing the stress on the limbs reduced the noise and the harshness to acceptable levels. This also reduced the performance level slightly.

Draw Weights

With any compound or cam bow, you will be able to shoot close to 10 pounds heavier draw weight than with a recurve, simply because it is easier to draw the bow past the increased peak weight at mid-draw than it is to hold the original weight at full draw.

In other words, it is easier to draw 60 pounds and hold 30 than it is to draw and hold 50. This factor helps the compound seem faster in some archers' minds, for they unconsciously end up comparing a 60-pound compound against a 50-pound recurve, as an example, and that's an unfair comparison. The heavier draw weight which now can be shot enables you to use a slightly heavier arrow than used before, and still have the desired speed and mass weight for improved kinetic energy, which helps arrow penetration.

Most hunting bow draw weights are 45 pounds on up, with 40 pounds considered the practical minimum for deer (in many states it's the legal minimum, too). Fifty-five pounds is generally considered a practical minimum draw weight for the hunting of larger, sturdier game such as bear, elk, etc. Be sure to check the regulations in the areas you plan to hunt to see just what the minimum requirements are.

Remember that with compounds, peak draw weight is peak draw weight, but with recurves the draw weight keeps on increasing as you pull back on the string. Standard increase is $2-2^1/_2$ pounds per inch, so a bow listed at 50 pounds weight at 28 inches would probably be 54-55 pounds of draw weight at 30 inches of draw. Conversely, at 26 inches of draw, it would only be 45-46 pounds.

Grips

Some bows—compounds and recurves—are made with interchangeable grips for high, medium or low wrist position. If the bow you like doesn't have this feature, the grip can be built up with tape, plastic wood, foam and tape, etc.

Pricing Bows

Bow prices vary considerably, depending on the style of a bow and its fanciness, and whether it is custom-made or production manufactured. Recurves can be found for $20-$30 all the way up to $400 or so for custom bows. Compounds range anywhere from around $75 to $500 or so for a top-of-the-line target bow, but most

The traditional compound design, right, has been improved with elongated eccentric wheels called cams.

that will accommodate the hunter's needs sell for $100-$200. If you are beginning in bowhunting, you would be wise to check your local pro-shop's used bow display. Prices are usually excellent there, and since you're just beginning you want to save your nickels for the bow you will most likely select once you have learned enough about shooting form and archery to make an intelligent choice.

Where should you buy your bow? Depends on how much service you will want. Obviously the more service you think you'll need, the closer aligned with a knowledgeable local retailer you should be.

Which Bow?

What draw weight should you get? There's only one answer, that's the draw weight you can handle confidently for the shooting of many arrows in one session. Not the heaviest draw weight you can draw once, but which you can handle for many arrows, drawing it with relative ease and aiming it with *control* and releasing the bowstring when you want to instead of when it pulls free from your hand.

The most common mistake archers make when choosing a bow is to buy one with too heavy a draw weight. Part of this mistake is caused by ego, the macho effect, and part by lack of knowledge. You can't grow into a bow if you can't handle it from the outset. Fathers often buy a too-heavy bow for their son and answer any suggestions with "He'll grow into it." What they are actually saying is, "I don't want to spend the money to get the right bow now and then spend more money to get another bow later.''

You must have a light enough draw weight that you can work with it easily as you practice countless shots to develop your shooting form and skills. It is far better to choose a bow that may seem a bit light, and then go to a heavier bow as your skills and strength improve, than it is to start with the maximum draw weight you can handle. After all, this is meant to be fun, and you have nothing to prove to anyone other than yourself.

Limit the draw weight to something you can handle *under the worst* conditions when you're cold and wet, and your muscles are weak. Then you know you'll always be able to take any shot that presents itself.

Remember your own height and arm length when selecting a bow. Shorter people generally can shoot short and medium length bows with less finger pinch and fewer drawing problems than taller, longer-armed people.

Weight In Hand, Handles

Mass weight, or weight in hand, of the bow is another important consideration. Bows with heavier physical weight rest more solidly in your hand at full draw and thus can be shot a bit more accurately than a light mass weight bow. On the other hand, the heavier the mass weight the more ounces you have to carry around all day. What's best? Whatever you prefer.

Handle material affects your choice, too. Magnesium alloy handles are light and strong. Aluminum alloy handles are too. Main thing with handle material is its feel in your bow hand in cold weather. Metal conducts heat away faster than wood. If you prefer the metal handle, tape foam or a leather pad over it and wear a glove.

Bowstrings

Most bowstrings today are made of Dacron. Some are made of Kevlar, and some are a mix of the two. There undoubtedly will be new and improved string materials on the market as time passes, but these products have proven satisfactory. Kevlar can be brittle. It's best features are that it stretches less than Dacron, is stronger and needs fewer strands per string, which makes a lighter string which provides less air drag when it is released.

Lighter draw weight bows most efficiently use a string with fewer strands; heavier draw weight bows need more strands in the bowstring to withstand the added shock.

Some hunters chose the longbow for the shooting challenge it provides and for the sake of nostalgia.

Standard recommendations for the best Dacron strings are: *20-30 pound bow, eight strands; 25-35 pound bow, 10 strands; 35-45 pound bow, 12 strands; 45-55 pound bow, 14 strands; 55-80 pound bow, 16 strands.* These are guidelines, not gospel. If you think it would help your particular shooting situation to adjust up or down a strand count, feel free to do so.

Most bowstrings are served with nylon at the loops and in the middle where the arrow will be nocked and your fingers or release will be positioned. Monofilament is also used. It won't fray like nylon will, but if it is not glued properly, it will work loose and unwind swiftly.

Always set up, shoot in (so it will shoot like the string on your bow) and carry with you a spare bow string when you go afield. Strands can become frayed or accidentally cut. You don't want to have to run back to camp if that happens. Beeswax rubbed regularly on the bowstring will help keep it from fraying and in good shape longer.

Bowstringers are available for use with compounds and for use with recurves. Recurve bowstringers hook over the limb tips;

compound bow stringers hook over the swaged unit at the end of the cable, onto which the bowstring will be hooked. Use a bowstringer when stringing and unstringing any bow, and when changing strings. There are other methods of stringing and unstringing recurves, but the bowstringer is the most secure and least likely to lead to a twisted limb.

Nock Set

The nocking point locator (positioned above the nock if you use only one) must be secure, but not so tight that it could weaken string strands, and it needs to be small enough to be out of the way of your fingers. Most common style is an open metal hoop with a rubber lining which is fitted over the string at the proper position and clamped firmly with a special nock pliers.

A nock set above and below the arrow nock creates a firmer setting. Some people put two nock sets above the arrow nock and one below as their security. This makes it easy to slip a nock onto the string without looking (such as if you are watching a game animal) and slide the nock up against the nock set.

When you're beginning to set up and tune a new bow, make several wraps with adhesive tape or wind thread around the string at the estimated best point. This setup is easy to change if needed. Then mark the right height with the metal clip.

Arrow Rest

The arrow rest needs to support the arrow vertically and horizontally before the shot, but it must not cause any drag on the arrow when it is shot. When a bow is properly set up and tuned, the arrow should jump slightly up and to the side from the arrow rest.

Rests must be *strong* and *quiet*. If they are adjustable, and some of the newer, more expensive ones are, you have added benefits.

Hunting rests today vary all the way from a "rug" rest which is nothing more than a strip of carpet-like material glued on the sight window shelf, to high adjustable devices mounted in the cushion plunger hole with support arms of various configurations and materials. This latter type is the maximum development of the reliable finger-type arrow rest, made of wire or plastic or wire coated with plastic, which offers vertical and lateral support, but also has enough give that it can negate various improper pressures applied to the arrow when you draw. There can be too much side pressure or too much downward pressure from the top finger of the drawing hand.

No matter which style of arrow rest you use, be certain that the contact points on the side plate or cushion plunger and on the arrow rest do not become hard. When that happens, your arrow is more likely to squeal as it is drawn. That violin imitation isn't well received in the hunting woods by wild game or by bowhunters.

How To Find Your Draw Length

You can determine your draw length in a variety of ways.

Nock a full length arrow shaft (32 inches) on a light draw weight bow and draw it back to your anchor point. (Anchor point is the place on your face your hand stops every time you reach full draw.) Have an observer mark on the shaft the point at which the shaft meets the front of the bow handle. Measure the distance from the mark to the bottom of the nock slot, or string groove, in the nock. This will approximate your target shooting draw length.

Remember, hunting arrows must be 1-1$^1/_2$ inches longer than target arrows. A target arrow point can be drawn back past the front of the bow because it is the same, or nearly the same diameter as the outside diameter of the shaft. A broadhead's blades prevent it from being drawn that far. The broadhead blades should not be drawn back against the front of the bow, because they could click and attract an animal's attention or they could knock the arrow off the rest. The additional length also prevents the broadhead from cutting the fingers of your bowhand.

For the experienced archer, this method of determining draw length works well, but it can be inaccurate for a beginner, simply because the new archer's shooting form is not developed, muscles are not trained to properly draw the bow, etc. The basic unfamiliarity with all of it could produce an inaccurate reading unless you have a knowledgeable person helping.

Another method of measuring draw length is to butt one end of a yard stick against the middle of your chest and stretch out the fingertips of both hands as far as you can on the yard stick. The distance from chest to fingertips is close to your draw length. But your arrows must be at least $^1/_2$-inch longer.

A third method is to stand roughly an arm's-length from a wall at right angles so that you are looking straight ahead and parallel to the wall. Make a fist and extend your arm nearest the wall so that the part of your fingers between your first and second knuckles lie flat against the wall. Turn your head so you are looking at the wall and your fist. Have someone measure the distance from the wall to the corner of your mouth.

There are a wide variety of arrow rests available to the hunter. They range from simple plastic "shelves" to complicated devices with lots of bells and whistles. All have advantages.

With this system, left hand shooters should put their right fist against the wall and measure to the left corner of their mouth. Right hand shooters should place their left fist against the wall and measure to the right corner of their mouth.

Now that you know your approximate draw length, you can select the compound bow set for your draw length, or know what draw weight you will encounter when drawing a recurve to that length (allowing for plus/minus poundage according to the plus/minus distance your draw length is from 28 inches, as explained earlier.)

Determining Appropriate Draw Weight

Forty-five to 50 pounds draw weight is a decent starting point for average or larger men. Women ought to start at 30-35 pounds. Teen-age boys and smaller men would probably be most comfortable starting in the 40-45 pound area. The only reliable way to determine *your* best starting weight is to try bows of different draw weights.

Your ultimate draw weight goal will be determined by the

The simplest way to determine accurate draw length is with a special arrow shaft marked at one inch increments.

animals you intend to hunt. As noted earlier, moose, elk and such have thicker skins and larger bones than do deer and pronghorn. There is no short cut, you simply need to develop the strength to shoot the necessary draw weight.

Do not make the mistake of thinking that shooting a heavier draw weight bow automatically means you will be shooting a faster arrow. Nothing could be further from the truth, but this is a common misconception. Bow/arrow combinations vary widely! Not all bows of equal weight store the same energy; not all are equally efficient once that energy is released.

Besides, as draw weight of the bow increases, arrow weight and stiffness must increase correspondingly to be properly matched. Kinetic energy definitely will increase, but beyond that too many variables come into play: arrow length, broadhead weight, arrow speed, energy stored, bow efficiency, tuning effect (good or poor), string release from fingers or mechanical release, etc.

Here is some information gleaned from data recorded at a Wisconsin Bowhunters Association autumn broadhead shoot. I think you'll find it interesting!

The most important factor to note here is the wide range of high and low kinetic energy numbers within each 10-pound draw weight bracket. Note that the highest kinetic energy number for the 40-49 pound bracket was only $3\frac{1}{2}$ foot-pounds below the low number for the 70-79 pound bracket! Note that the kinetic energy range for the 60-69 pound draw bracket was 40 foot-pounds, an incredible range which serves to point out that any setup's performance is a condition of many factors, and a blanket assumption is dangerous.

3

The Right Arrows
For Your Bow

We buy a bow, then ask, "Ok, now what arrows should I use?"

Good question. There is a variety of materials, and an even wider variety in sizes and stiffnesses. Arrow manufacturers have charts to guide you, and they are a great help.

The arrow is the most critical part of your setup. It is the indicator, the final result, as it flies down-range. Good arrows, *matched properly*, will shoot well from any bow. Poor arrows, or good arrows matched improperly, won't fly well from any bow.

Shaft Materials

Shafts are made of tubular aluminum, tubular fiberglass, solid wood (Port Orford cedar, sometimes compressed, sometimes not), and tubular carbon/aluminum. Solid fiberglass and tubular steel arrows are used for bowfishing.

Tubular Aluminum. All target and field shooters use tubular aluminum. Most bowhunters use tubular aluminum. This shaft is the most consistent in construction, shaft to shaft, and is strong and light. When bent, it can be straightened if it isn't beyond the point of no return. It has the widest variety of shaft sizes, which permits the closest matching of shaft to bow and shooter. There also is a wider range of shaft quality than many bowhunters realize.

Tubular Fiberglass. Tubular fiberglass is very consistent in generally are heavier in grain weight than aluminum, comparing stiffness to stiffness.

Wood. Wood shafts cannot be as consistent in structure, shaft to shaft, simply because we have no control over the growth of the tree that produced the wood. Wood shafts are light and inexpensive, and are straight enough for hunting uses but not for the ultimate target uses. Wood arrows usually can be straightened when they take a crooked set, but not always. Grain structure must be considered when nocks are attached to be certain that energy forces from the bow are applied properly. At one angle, the grain is less flexible than at another angle.

Cedar is used because of its straight grain characteristics and high tendency to remain straight when milled. Consistency of shaft can be helped some by compressing the cedar shaft. This also makes it more dense and thus heavier for its outside diameter. Overall, it is a good shaft, but just not as consistent in straightness, stiffness or weight as other materials.

Solid Fiberglass & Tubular Steel. Solid fiberglass and tubular steel shafts are too heavy for hunting use. They are useful only for short-range shots encountered in bowfishing. Their mass gives them good water penetration characteristics.

Carbon/Aluminum. Carbon/aluminum shafts are a specialty item for a few target archers. This is a light, strong shaft—and a finished dozen of them will cost right around $250!

Tubular Fiberglass/Graphite. Tubular fiberglass/graphite arrows were available a few years ago but appear to have dropped from the scene due to quality-control problems.

Price

What will you pay for finished hunting arrows? Wood arrows will be mostly in the $12-$25 per dozen range. Fiberglass in the $30-$40 range. Aluminum hunting arrows will range from $15 to $60, depending upon the type of alloy used and the hardness of that alloy. Generally, the harder the alloy the more punishment it will take, but this varies with each alloy.

Some of the hardest alloys, used for target arrows only, are too brittle for hunting use and will break instead of bending slightly.

Price must be your main guidance on shaft quality until you learn more about them. You might want to remember that the least expensive ones are known as ''one-shotters'' in the trade, meaning that there's a good chance the shaft will bend on the first shot and not be repairable. The lower quality alloys do not have a

Though many types of arrows will work for the hunter, only trial and error and recommendations from veteran hunters will help you determine the best type for you.

Aluminum shafts are available mostly in orange anodized finish and camo green, brown or gray finish.

Basics of Arrow Physics

The term "straight as an arrow" is misleading. An arrow at rest is straight, but when the bowstring is released that arrow swiftly bends left and right in a series until it straightens out in flight a short distance beyond the bow. This bending is known as "paradox."

The bending can be helpful, for it aids the arrow in clearing the bow and the cables in the case of a compound. For best performance, this bending needs to be held to the proper amount; there can be too little as well as too much bending. Correct bending occurs when the arrow is properly matched to the rest of the setup.

On bows that are not cut to full centershot, the tip of the arrowpoints a fraction of an inch off center. The arrow doesn't shoot off to the side because the string is trying to push it straight ahead.

The released bowstring rolls off your fingertips to the left if you are a right-handed shooter and to the right if you are a left-handed shooter. The laws of physics require an equal reaction for every action, so the string in its attempt to push the arrow straight ahead swings back and forth across the line of thrust as it moves forward. It rotates back to static brace height in a rough "S" movement.

The nock of the arrow, which receives the sudden shock of energy being released, must move with the bowstring to the left of center for right-handed shooters, right of center for left-handed shooters. As forward limb pressure, through the bowstring, tries to pull everything back into true center, the arrow tip is pushed right (right-handed shooter) into the arrow rest side plate, which resists this pressure.

The major part of the arrow shaft is free to bend between the rear and forward pressure points, which it does. The degree of bend is controlled by the shaft stiffness, referred to as "spine."

A heavier spine will bend less, but will recover more slowly. An arrow will not straighten out into true flight until about 20 yards down range, but it will have basically dampened the bending within 10 yards. Before it reaches this point, the arrow goes through about $2^1/_2$ bends to clear the bow and several dampened bends as it flies. One left bend and one right bend constitutes a "cycle."

The fractional beginning of the second right bend helps move the fletching away from the arrow rest, thus clearing the bow.

A properly shot arrow should touch the arrow rest for as short a distance as possible after the launch. The arrow rest thus cannot exert a drag on the arrow, and the arrow is more free to recover properly with better speed.

The string continues to accelerate the arrow until well past the mid-range of limb recovery, but since the arrow is in motion the bending of the arrow will be less because there is less resistance from a moving object than from a stationary object. The controlling effects of the fletching, arrow spine and air friction will continue the dampening of the arrow's bending.

The centershot bow is designed to minimize these deflections by allowing the arrow to be positioned as nearly as possible in the same direction of thrust as the bowstring.

Nocks

Arrow nocks are available with straight inner line or snap-on string slots. The straight inner line nocks are of two types—the

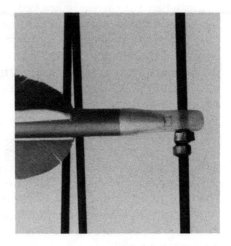

The importance of every detail right down to the nock can not be overlooked if you expect consistent performance from your arrows.

"speed" nock with straight outer lines and a small ridge on the outer surface which corresponds to the cock feather position so you can properly nock the arrow on the string without looking at it, and the smaller, tapered-outer-edge nocks that many serious target archers use. The smaller nock offers less opportunity for your fingers accidentally to pinch the nock and restrict arrow flight.

Snap-on nocks have a slightly smaller string slot than the other nocks, with an enlarged circle at the base of the slot in which the string seats. The outer diameter is flattened some horizontally top and bottom to fit better between your fingers. The snap-on type holds the arrow on the string better when you move your fingers away.

For hunting, you will be most happy with snap-on nocks.

Snap-on nocks must fit snugly, but not too tightly on the bowstring. A nock that is too tight will hold the arrow on the string longer than it should upon the shot and thus will rob the arrow of some of its energy and speed, creating a more arched trajectory.

Nocks are available in several sizes to fit best on different shaft sizes and different bowstring thicknesses.

Fletching

Fletching is the rudder that guides the arrow. At least that's its purpose. If the fletching is too small or applied too straight, the broadhead can take over flight control, with disastrous results.

Most arrows have three fletches—two hen fletches, the outer edges of which align vertically with the bow's sight window and string when the arrow is nocked, and a cock feather which sits at right angle to the sight window, pointing away from it.

Bowhunters who do a lot of stillhunting and stalking probably will use darker fletches to help avoid detection. Tree stand hunters most likely will use lighter, brighter fletching to help in hit identification. A lighter tone is less easy to see against a mottled background of branches and sky.

Arrows with four fletches have those fletches glued in a 75/105 degree arrangement or a consistent 90 degree setup, usually the former because clearance is easier. The idea is that four fletches will not need to be as large to have the same stabilizing effect as three fletches and should make it easier to achieve good clearance. Also, in the excitement of nocking another arrow when a second shot is offered, with four fletches you don't need to look at the fletching to be sure the arrow is nocked properly. It cannot be nocked incorrectly.

The design you choose comes back to personal preference. Three fletch systems use five or five-and-one-half inch fletches. Four-fletch systems use four-inch fletches. The fletches in a three-fletch system are 120 degrees apart, and from my experience provide no less or no more clearance. Other factors are more important in achieving necessary clearance. The fletches must be large enough to provide enough drag and mounted with enough curve to provide necessary spin stabilization. Otherwise, a head probably will plane off course.

Fletching can be applied straight down the shaft (least amount of control due to least spin imparted), straight offset, which is a straight fletch glued at an angle (medium control), or helical, which has a slight twist given to the fletch as it is glued at an angle on the shaft. The helical gives the most flight stability and control because it imparts the most spin stabilization to the shaft. It is the fletch attachment style bowhunters should use.

Flu-flu is a fourth fletching system designed for maximum air drag and short arrow flight. It is used for wing shooting at birds and hand-thrown targets. The flu-flu can be made by winding one uncut feather around the shaft, or by using four to six extra large, untrimmed feathers in helical style. My personal preference is to set up the fletching jig for six fletches but to omit the sixth fletch. With the nock properly aligned, this gap lies closest to the sight window and gives the best clearance.

All fletches will have a parabolic or shield trim. Nearly all fletches today are parabolic. The vacuum which develops behind the shield cut increases drag and causes the rear part of the feather to lie down somewhat in flight, decreasing its stabilizing ability.

Vanes Or Fletches

Fletches are made of turkey feathers or plastic vanes. Each has its adherents. Feathers are lighter weight, have a rougher surface to create more air turbulence and thus more stability, and are more forgiving because they push easily out of the way when struck by cable, arrow rest or twig.

Vanes are quieter and resistant to moisture. You don't hear a noise when you accidentally scrape your jacket sleeve against a plastic fletch.

Feathers can be waterproofed by spraying them with dry-fly dope. Some bowhunters put a plastic bag over feather fletching on arrows in a quiver when hunting in damp weather.

Fletches are glued to the shaft in left wing or right wing style. Left wings curve left on helical style and right wings curve right. They impart spin in the same directions. It is not highly critical which you use, because clearance is about equal. However, some shooters have noticed they get a bit better clearance if they match the wing side with their shooting side, i.e., right wing for right hand shooting. They also found this gives less wear on the lower hen fletch. Sometimes a slight change in nock rotation will solve the clearance problem, as will raising or lowering the nock location on the bowstring. Feathers are rough on one side and smooth on the other. The rough side sets up air turbulence which helps stabilization. When you fletch arrows, just be sure that you don't mix left and right wing feathers on a shaft.

Points

Archery has six basic point styles for arrows: *broadhead (hunting), target, field, blunt, fish* and *bird*.

Broadhead

Broadheads are bladed heads for hunting small game, birds, varmints and big game. Some hunters prefer not to use them for small game, but that is strictly personal choice. Broadheads have a center ferrule made of metal or plastic, almost always metal, with two to six blades attached. (Some states do not allow plastic-ferrule broadheads.)

Most broadhead models and styles weigh between 120 and 150 grains, but some exist at each end of the range. Weight is a factor of construction, blade number, etc., but it also is an important factor to remember when matching arrows to your setup and in tuning for best flight.

Any weight at the front of the arrow shaft acts as resistance when energy is applied at the nock end. The heavier the broadhead the more resistance. The more resistance encountered, the more the arrow shaft will bend, in effect "softening" it or making it act less stiff. As little as 10 grains difference can produce a change. Since too much and too little bending cause mismatching, the weight of the broadhead definitely affects equipment matching. Most errors are made by placing too much weight on the front of the arrow, softening the shaft's stiffness.

Ferrules are glued on a five-degree taper of the arrow shaft or a glued-in insert, or a threaded base is constructed as part of the ferrule, which is then screwed into a threaded insert glued in the forward end of the arrow shaft. The right type of hot-melt ferrule cement should be available at any retail store carrying archery equipment.

The screw-in style is the most popular by far because of its versatility. A dull broadhead can be screwed out and quickly replaced by a sharp one....field points can replace broadheads for plinking or other practice....Judo Points can replace field points if you're going to wander through the woods for practice shooting at random targets at unknown distances. The Judo Point is a blunt point with spring-loaded wires added, which snag brush, grass, etc., upon impact and instantly stop arrow flight.

Which Broadhead?

You have a wide range of good broadheads to choose from. We all have different preferences—number of blades, screw-in or glue on, solid blade versus vented blade, grain weight, blade point or punch point, fixed blades or replaceable blades, and not all broadheads fly equally well for everyone. In fact, not all broadheads fly equally well for any individual equipment setup.

Some bowhunters like a two-bladed head, feeling that it has a better chance of slipping between the ribs of a big game animal. At best, there is maybe only a 50/50 chance to begin with. At worst, only one blade angle doesn't cut enough skin and muscle to produce as good a blood trail as desired. Besides, with the heavier draw weights generally shot today, because of compound bows, the "avoid the ribs" concern is not what it used to be, except for the larger big game species where it will always be a concern.

While both one-piece and replacable blade broadhead models are available to the hunter, the latter are usually preferred today.

A head with three or more blades is preferred. Skin pulls back better from such a cut compared to a two-blade, single-angle head, and since muscle layers under the skin lie at angles with one another (cross-striation) the multiple-blade head does more effective cutting there, too. A single blade might cut across one grain, letting the filaments pull back, but might slip with the grain on another layer and leave a hole which would essentially remain closed because of continued muscle fiber tension.

Sometimes the entry hole in the skin can slip back or ahead of the entry hole through the muscle and into the vitals, because the animal may have had a leg forward or back at the instant of the hit. This movement can block off a wound and reduce or stop a blood trail. The larger and more circular that entry hole the better is the chance of a good blood trail, and an opening created by a multi-blade head becomes circular quickly.

Shoot a multi-blade head and a two-blade head at a styrofoam target. My experience has been that the multi-bladed head is much easier to pull from the target. I believe this is because the additional edge makes a more open cut and reduces the gripping effect. Foam isn't constructed like muscle tissue, but there's something working in favor of the multi-bladed head here that also translates to use on animal targets.

Most replaceable blades are 20/1000ths of an inch thick or thicker. This gives a sturdier blade which will hold a razor sharp edge *and* is more resistant when glancing off or needing to penetrating bone.

There always will be debate on the merits of a point which has sharp blades all the way forward to the tip, versus the conical tip versus the pyramid-shaped tip. A blade which extends all the way to the tip begin cutting immediately and takes less pounds of pressure to make a hole than does a punch-type head, but it has proven an impractical style for replaceable blade heads. The pyramid-shaped tip is an excellent middle ground because it has edges which begins to cut with less force than required by the purely conical point. The conical or pyramid-shaped point on replaceable-blade heads adds needed strength.

If you plan to hunt the larger big game, be certain that you have a strong broadhead, whether it is of replaceable-blade style or fixed blade style. Some outfitters will not allow thin-bladed heads, or some styles of broadheads, fearing that the head will come apart on impact. Check with your outfitter when planning such a hunt.

Field Points

Field points are made in screw-in or glue-on style, usually used by bowhunters for practice sessions. They have a shouldered design as opposed to a bullet or conical point. Most field points are 125 grains or 145 grains. Use these to practice with, matching the field point as closely as possible to your broadhead weight, but remember to do your final bow tuning with broadheads to be sure they fly right.

Target Points

Target points are small, bullet or conically-tipped points used only for target shooting.

Blunts

Blunts are made of flat-ended metal, hard plastic or hard rubber. Plastic and rubber blunts usually have a wider leading-edge diameter than base diameter, simply to have better opportunity to develop a shocking impact instead of penetration. Flat-tipped steel blunts are great for stump shooting because they punch a hole

A safe test for broadhead sharpness is to run the edge on the blade across a semi-taut rubber band.

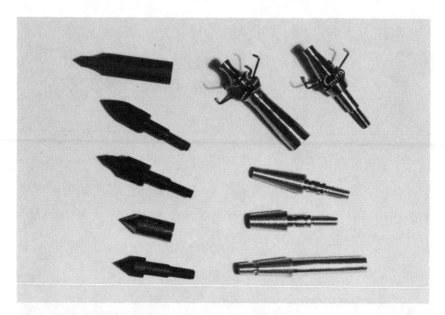

Target points and Judo points are best for off season practice, but always be sure to practice with broadheads before you hunt with them.

instead of wedging tightly. They are much easier to remove.

Fish Points

Bowfishing points have barbs, fixed or retractable, and are flat or conically tipped.

Bird Heads

Bird heads have wire loops or oversized prongs pointing out from the ferrule. The purpose, of course, is to have a larger impact surface area. Birds, especially flying birds, provide little resistance to impact, and feathers are tough. For these reasons, many bowhunters use broadheads instead of bird heads when after pheasants or grouse, and always for turkeys. Of course, since most birds are shot incidentally to big game hunting, the broadhead naturally will be used there.

4

The Right Sights & Accessories For Your Rig

Most bowhunters use bowsights these days. Sights help us shoot more accurately with less practice than required for good instinctive (barebow) shooting. There are pin sights, pendulum sights and rangefinding sights.

Sights are attached to the bow with screws at the mounting holes on the side of the bow handle opposite the sight window, or are taped on. Some mount on the front of the sight window, which is more easily done on wood handle bows.

The standard sight consists of a frame with one or two slots for the sight pins and four or five pins. Western bowhunters generally have more pins on their sight than do brush country and woodlot hunters because Westerners generally have much more opportunity for shots at a wider range of distances.

Sights usually are set in 10-yard increments, such as 10, 20, 30, 40 and 50, or 20 through 60. Some sights with a few more bells and whistles will automatically, more or less, help set mid-range sight pins if you set the maximum and minimum distance pins.

Pendulum sights are designed for use from treestands. The sight pin mounting pivots as the bow is lowered or raised, depending upon the distance the target is from your stand. Properly sighted in, this eliminates the need to judge the distance; the pendulum effect does that for you. Most of these sights require sighting in from a specific height above ground level. Some of the newer models have an internal pendulum and multiple pin fiber optics which brighten or dim as the bow is raised or lowered.

Rangefinding sights are seldom seen. They usually required bracketing of some sort. These systems didn't work as well as planned, apparently.

Judging distance accurately is more difficult than we tend to believe, as tests done by the Army and others have shown. There is no substitute for practice, of course, but a rangefinding optical aid can be invaluable. You won't use it to estimate the range to an animal within shooting range, but you can and should use it to check distances to various points at which you expect game to appear. This is especially helpful when you are hunting from a ground blind or treestand because you're in a fixed position. This tool is just as helpful, though, in larger country or when you are moving — simply because you can never check distances and practice distance judging too much.

The entire bit of distance judging always is a thorn. An arrow's trajectory is more than we think it is because we usually launch the arrow at a slightly upward slope instead of absolute horizontal. Our reference from eye to target may be horizontal, but the nock of the arrow is below our eye.

One interesting solution, or attempted solution, is to use only one or two sight pins, setting them at roughly 20 and 40 yards. Applying a bit of fudge factor, these two pins eliminate a lot of sight pin confusion and can be estimated just as accurately as a multitude of pins.

Remember that an arrow is rising in the first several yards of a shot and that the trajectory is higher than our mind wants to believe. This knowledge comes in handy when you want to shoot at an animal but there is an obstruction, such as a fallen log, between you and the intended target. If you have practiced, you will know whether you can put your sight pin on the animal's vitals, even if you need to look "through" the obstruction, and have the arrow pass above the obstruction and drop down into the desired spot on the target.

If you shoot with sights, there may be a time when you don't want to use them—such as shooting straight down or at an extremely close target. In this instance, try shifting your string hand so all fingers are under the arrow, then moving your anchor up to your cheekbone so you are looking right down the arrow. This is known as "gunbarreling," and it is handy to have practiced.

Sights come in a variety of configurations with various range finding and elevation compensation options. To make the best choice, consider the type and location of the hunting you'll be doing most.

To adjust a sight, remember that you have a front sight and a rear sight, but the situation is opposite that of a firearm. On a firearm, the front sight is fixed and the rear sight is adjustable. On a bow, the front sight (the sight pin on your bow) is adjustable and the rear sight (your anchor point and head angle) is *fixed*!

To correct errors as you are shooting, move the sight pin *to the error*. For instance, if your arrow group is high and left, move your sight pin high and left. This will bring the arrow rest down and to the right.

Quivers

You need a quiver to carry arrows. The fellow who buys a bow and one arrow because "that's all I'll need," or a handful of arrows which he intends to carry in his hand, is not a figment of a retail shop operator's imagination, but he ought to be.

The quiver must cover and protect the broadheads with a hood silently, carry enough of them, and not be an obstruction. The large cover, or hood, is partially filled with foam and protects blade edges from brush and anything else which could dull the edge. It protects you, bowstrings of other bows and such from the sharp blades. In some states a quiver that covers broadheads is mandatory for hunting!

You will find bow quivers, back quivers and hip quivers.

Bow quivers attach to the bow, usually at the same place the sight attaches. It's a good idea to put rubber bushings between the mounting plates in such a case, so the screws hold more tightly. The quiver should be mounted so the hood is up and nocks down. This keeps debris out of the hood and makes it easier to push the bow ahead of you through brush.

If the quiver is vertically adjustable, mount it at a position which keeps the arrow nocks off the ground and the entire unit, filled with arrows, balances well when you lift the bow to draw and aim. (Incidentally, a bow with a bow quiver might shoot arrows to a slightly different point of impact than one without a bow quiver, so if you will hunt with a bow quiver practice that way.)

The hood must be large enough to accept the number of broadheads it was designed to hold without the blades touching. The quiver's lower clip must hold the arrows snugly but not so snugly they are difficult to remove, and the slots must be positioned slightly fanned so the fletches do not rub together. If the rubber is too soft, thin screws screwed into the rubber between each clip may tighten the spacing and help the clip hold the arrows more snugly.

Mount the clip as low as possible. Don't clip arrows near mid-length but close to the fletches. This keeps them from catching on brush and popping free or bending. It also keeps fletches from vibrating against each other when you shoot.

Quivers generally hold four to eight arrows, depending upon the design. A four-arrow quiver usually is enough for brush country bowhunters, but Western hunters like to carry as many arrows as possible because they often get more shooting.

Back quivers are made in two styles, the old leather kind that Robin Hood used and which Howard Hill preferred, called a shoulder quiver, and a hooded design which rides fairly low in the middle of your back.

The leather bag holds plenty of arrows, but broadheads can bump together easily and lose their edge unless you fill the bottom with soft material. Whole grain oats work; so does uncooked

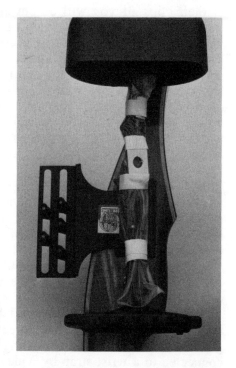

Today's most common quiver attaches directly to the bow. It keeps arrows quiet and heads clean. The author stores a spare bowstring in a plastic bag taped to the stem of his quiver.

oatmeal. The heads nest in this layer and are fairly well protected.

Those who like this quiver say the arrows are protected by your head and neck when you move through brush. Those who don't particularly like to reach over their shoulder for an arrow and who don't want fletchings rubbing and scraping have less-kind words for it.

I hunted bears with a longbow enthusiast once. He used this style quiver and proved that, if you practice, you can develop a fast rhythm to pull arrows. He hit a nice boar on the bait with his first shot, and the bear walked away instead of running. In the time it took the bear to walk 20 yards, John had three more arrows into him.

"I didn't want it to get away," John said, "so I kept shooting until it went down."

The best back quivers will hold up to a dozen arrows snugly in clips. The hood covers broadheads and keeps them well protected. Some designs have a small pack above the hood for gear storage, an extra jacket, etc. Arrows are removed easily and with little noticeable motion simply by reaching back and slipping them out of their clips. If you will be out all day and anticipate plenty of shooting, this can be an excellent second quiver, supplementing the arrows you carry in a bow quiver.

The hip or belt quiver holds arrows point down and nock end up in clips, with foam in the cup to hold the broadheads securely. You can reach an arrow fairly easily without looking for it, but the exposed fletches pointing upward can be noisy to try to get through brush. They aren't always as well protected by your back as you want them to be. This style generally is made to hold five to eight arrows.

Finger Tabs And Gloves, Armguards

Anyone who shot bows in physical education classes or at camp as a youngster remembers the sore fingers and arm welts more than anything else. Seldom was any thrill or satisfaction involved with the shooting.

It is not macho to shoot without this protection, it is foolhardy. Anticipated arm bruises and sore fingers make you flinch more quickly than anything.

Finger protection is provided by tabs which slip over your second finger and protect the three string fingers, or by shooting gloves which actually are nothing more than three finger stalls connected to a wrist strap by wide elastic or leather strips.

Tabs are made of leather or plastic. Leather tabs are either smooth or covered with calf hair. Some archers feel they get a smoother release with a calf hair tab, and some don't. Tabs will have one, two or three layers and are available in various sizes. One layer is alright for light draw weight bows, but for hunting weights use tabs with two or three layers to get the protection needed.

Some tabs have a spacer which fits between the index finger and second finger. The spacer's purpose is to keep you from pinching the nock too tightly between those two fingers.

Shooting gloves are made of leather or vinyl, usually leather. The finger stalls cover your string fingers back to the second knuckle, or slightly forward of that.

Use whichever style you prefer. I prefer a tab because it is easier to use and doesn't chill the ends of my string hand fingers in cold weather. Leather stalls on shooting gloves seem to draw the heat from your fingers. Stalls which don't fit snugly enough twist easily on your finger. Stalls seem to groove more easily than tabs; a groove is unwanted because it causes the bowstring to hang up slightly on release. A sloppy release of this nature can make you pluck the string unintentionally. A tab is easy to use with regular gloves; simply slice the base of the second finger of your string hand glove, insert the tab's finger loop and pull the glove on your hand.

Armguards are made in two basic lengths and in several styles. The hunting armguard style is long enough to cover your forearm and part of your upper arm. This extra length also helps keep your sleeve out of the string's path. It is the best armguard to use when you are learning, simply because it offers so much protection. The shorter armguard, which covers most of your forearm only, is mostly used by target and field shooters, but it can easily be worn while bowhunting.

Some armguards are solid; some are ventilated. The ventilated ones are the most comfortable in warm weather because they don't collect perspiration like the solid leather models will. Most of the ventilated armguards are made of plastic.

Armguards have adjustable elastic bands, with metal hooks or Velcro fasteners. The width is tapered. Be sure the widest width is closest to your elbow, with the narrowest width closest to your wrist.

If your sleeve is fairly snug, you may want to wear the armguard under the sleeve. This will give your skin the necessary protection, but the noise of a string hitting the fabric may be softer than when hitting bare leather or plastic. This is a minor concern. It is far better to have proper clearance so the bowstring hits nothing.

Arrow Holders

This little device is an unsung hero. It does exactly what its name says — it holds the arrow in position on the arrow rest until you begin to draw. You do not need to hold the arrow on the arrow rest with the index finger of your bow hand, nor do you want to because it is tiring. The real problem is that you unconsciously apply heavy, consistent downward pressure on the arrow rest as you hold the arrow in position with your finger. This unwanted pressure can bend the arrow rest finger or weaken it, either of which can cause poor performance or drop the arrow off the end of the arrow rest support finger at the worst possible time.

Air Flow Indicator

This is a fancy name for an eight-inch length of sewing thread

Though "cat whiskers," the rubber skirt device shown above, helps to silence the bow string, the threaded yarn shown higher on the string makes a more sensitive wind direction indicator. In some cases, it can even reveal the movement of thermals early and late in the day.

tied to your bow's upper limb tip and used as fast indicator of the direction of flow of a light breeze. It is not essential, but it can be valuable. *Always pay attention to wind direction.*

Bow Cases

Cases vary from a light cloth piece to a hard-shelled, rugged unit adequate for shipping bows and accessories by air, and they give a degree of protection relative to material used.

Light cloth zippered cases provide a minimum of protection, but they are handy to have when you want to keep the bow covered and clean, keep fletches on arrows in a bow quiver from getting dinged, etc. In states which require that a bow be unstrung or cased when in a vehicle and/or during non-hunting hours, these light cases handily fill the bill. Hunters keep the case with them, not removing their bow until they're on stand at legal hunting hours, and encasing the bow in the evening before leaving the stand.

Padded, zippered vinyl cases are excellent for general transportation. They give good protection, yet are not unduly bulky or heavy.

With the fabric or padded case, make sure your bowsight won't be damaged in transit. It can happen easily. Best way to prevent it is to use a bowsight which mounts and dismounts easily and simply remove it when casing the bow. There's usually little problem with a padded bow case and regular sized sight. Some of the larger sight and sight bracket setups must be removed each time the bow is cased.

Hard cases are usually plastic or aluminum, with good locks.

They must be baffled adequately inside so the shell cannot be pushed in, which could damage the contents.

If you wish, a custom case of plywood may be the ticket for serious travel, especially by air. The case can be built to your specifications to hold whatever equipment and other gear you wish.

If you are shipping gear anywhere, lock the locks and tape around the case and over each lock with duct tape or rugged fiber-lined tape. This is more of a deterrent to potential thieves working at shipping terminals and airports than to give added protection. Tampering with the tape can be noticeable, and if contents are missing the case obviously then will have been tampered with. Locks can accidentally fly open, but tape doesn't accidentally unwrap and rewrap.

A friend of mine once shipped two rifles by air in a hard case from his Alabama home to a western state. At his destination he picked his gun case off the freight delivery belt and headed for the back country. When he opened his case at camp, two bricks at each end of the case (roughly equal to the weight of the gear he had packed) greeted him.

"The people who took my guns had done it before, I believe," my friend said.

Packs

This category includes belt, fanny, day and backpacks. Each has different uses and is most practical in certain situations.

Belt packs are small. They are an updated version of the frontiersman's "possibles bag," because they are designed to carry small items possibly necessary for a myriad of reasons. Common items are an extra bowstring, light rope, knife, tissue paper or surveyor's tape for marking blood trails, plastic bag, spare nocks and glue, extra broadheads, small pliers, screwdriver, allen wrenches to fit the bow, spare arrow rest, moleskin (for bow silencing and foot care), tubes of camo grease, headnet, insect repellent, lure or masking scent, couple of tree steps, hand pruning shears, folding saw, first aid kit, emergency shelter (space blanket or sheet of plastic), roll of tape, etc.

It is easy to see why a larger pack may be needed.

Fanny packs belt around your waist and are supposed to ride at your waist or on your hips. They are large enough to carry much more gear than a belt pack, including extra clothes if needed. However, since they curve to fit your back, you cannot comfortably carry long rigid objects. Rectangular packs hold the most gear; the kidney-shaped ones look great, but the rounded shape eliminates corner storage and pushes everything into a lump in the middle and at the top. Heavy objects instantly settle to the bottom and bounce on your butt as you walk.

Any fanny pack should be attached to its belt on the long side for carrying ease and comfort. I had a fanny pack years ago which was roughly four inches by seven inches by 15 inches. The belt was sewn on the four-inch side, which made the pack stick out to the rear like a block...an uncomfortable, floppy block.

I am not a strong fan of fanny packs. They get in the way of other items carried on your pants belt, don't carry as much as they should, and a daypack can do a better job in comfort.

Daypacks are basically teardrop shape. They hold a lot of gear and clothes, and they ride well unless overloaded. The chest strap on a daypack is one of the most useless items I've ever seen; even though saddle cinches work on a horse, this just doesn't work the same. There is no bottom support, so overloading pulls the load down.

Daypacks are practical. They can be a godsend on long day trips, carrying extra clothes, first aid and emergency gear, extra hunting items which aren't needed enough to be on the bow or in your hand but when needed are really needed. Your shoulders may get a bit tired if the bag is overloaded, but this beats, hands down, the fanny pack flop.

Fanny packs and day packs can be hung out of the way in the tree when you are on stand or stashed under the seat behind your feet. The pack will be out of the way when you stand up.

Backpacks obviously are the heavy-duty workhorse of this group. In addition to your own gear, they will carry trophy heads and hides, boned out meat, etc. Be sure to take enough game bags and plastic bags if you plan to carry out meat, and load that weight high for easiest carrying. Remove bones because it is senseless to carry them out.

A few creative bowhunters have made a light metal frame which holds a daypack and a big fanny pack, and which rides on shoulder straps and hip belt. That load is versatile and rides easily. Once at camp, they can use part or all of this setup as their day-to-day hunting pack.

5

Treestands and Other Gear

Depending upon your point of view, tree stands are a necessity or a hindrance. If you hunt in tree and brush country, they can be wonderful—and a hindrance. If you hunt where there are no trees, they obviously are of no help. If you hunt timbered mountains, you are overlooking a good hunting tool if you dismiss treestands as Eastern or flatlander devices. Even if you hunt in areas where there are no trees large enough to hold treestands, elevated stands can be and are used frequently and successfully.

Treestands can get you above thick vegetation, allowing you to see down into it for a better view of trails and game.

Treestands can help get your alarming human scent far enough above the ground that game animals do not notice it or notice it so little they pay no attention to it.

Treestands can take you out of the primary line of vision of game animals and give you a bit more freedom to move when necessary.

Treestands can let you see farther into brush or other terrain than you would be able to see from ground level, helping you be better prepared when an animal moves into view and then into range.

Treestands can give you a delightful view of nature being nature, of squirrels and rabbits and raccoons and grouse and big game going about their daily doings, with you sitting up there out of the way and grinning.

These factors come into play no matter whether you are

watching a Georgia whitetail area, an Ontario bait for black bear, a quakie-filled mountain pass for mule deer or a big smelly elk wallow.

They are not, however, the be-all and end-all of hunting tools.

They can hurt you if you're not careful.

They can be a lot of extra weight and bulk to carry around.

They can keep you rooted to one spot when you might be better off moving around, doing more scouting, hunting other promising areas, learning more about the game in your area and where it moves and feeds and hides. And where it goes when human pressure on it builds.

Keith Monson, a North Dakota bowhunting buddy, likes to push deer on small drives. His area of North Dakota has trees only in river and creek bottoms and in shelterbelts. Keith has absolutely no patience, and his face gets red when he gets excited. It gets reddest when he speaks of treestands.

"In the right place, they can be fine. But most people haul a treestand into the woods, climb into it and sit there. They think they have scouted the area, but have they? What if conditions change? Their mind goes blank. They stop thinking. They stop figuring out ways to find the deer. They stop learning about the best ways to hunt deer, or whatever, in their hunting territory.

"If you're going to use them, don't let them tie you to a tree like a dog on a chain. Use them to hunt effectively, if you want, but don't confuse sitting in a tree with good hunting. It can be, but often it isn't."

He has a good point, one which bowhunters can overlook easily.

The flip side of this is the opinion that if you're hunting the mountains a treestand is of no help. Sure, you want to hunt down from above onto animals because that's smart, but it doesn't always need to be on foot. Treestand use is simply a stationary example of the same thing.

Several years ago a group of California bowhunters created quite a stir in an area near where I was hunting in Utah because they set up treestands before daylight in quakie patches at high passes. There they waited for mule deer to filter through on the way to their bedding.

The fact which really made the stir, of course, was that they shot a bunch of big bucks.

The treestand is not *the* hunting tool; it is *a* hunting tool. Employ it where it works well, and use it right.

A prime example of this is any bowhunter who carries a light, small stand as a daypack, some treesteps in the pack which is fastened to the underside of the stand's platform, a small saw and a hand pruning shears.

With these tools, which are collectively quite light, you can set up and get into a treestand almost anywhere you want, on the spur of the moment, at any time you want. Sometimes you don't even need the stand, such as when a big, beautiful white oak or a handsome pine tree, both good natural stands, pops into view at the right place.

This is particularly useful on in-season scouting forays, such as a morning or afternoon taken to devote specifically to check new areas, or areas which you feel will be better to hunt in a week or so. If you see something you like, there's all the reason in the world to set up and wait a couple of hours or however long you wish. It is a free country, and you never know when the animal you want might come traipsing along.

That's flexibility and maneuverability. You are outfitting yourself to take maximum advantage of the signs you see in the animal's home terrain.

Types of Stands

There are permanent stands and portable stands. There are natural stands and commercially produced stands. Among the portables, there are climbing, non-climbing, ladder, wedge and tower stands (although many of these tower stands are easily portable only if you're King Kong). There also are sling stands.

Permanent Stands. Permanent stands usually are quite comfortable. Beyond that, I have difficulty in figuring out just why I would use one — one of the humanly-constructed kind, that is. Boards and planks and nails and spikes in a tree root you to that particular spot too easily. "It's there. I might as well use it." The thing is also an eyesore unless it is in your backyard and kids are playing in it. A permanent stand gives away your carefully chosen hunting spot as surely as would a lettered sign. If you are the only one with permission to hunt this location, the worry of stand poaching doesn't exist. Then, if you have a particular place (or places) which year in and year out are good producers, you have good reason to put in permanent stands.

Anti-hunters have been known to sabotage such stands. So will weather and porcupines and large birds that select them to roost and defecate in.

On a Texas deer and dove hunt one October with Jim Dougherty, Russ Tinsley and Murray Burnham, I learned firsthand of this latter factor. I stood on the ground while Jim climbed the ladder to peek in an enclosed tower stand. This thing was the Hilton of tower stands.

Jim opened the door, let out a yelp, ducked and almost fell off the ladder. The owl which came shooting out the door past his shoulder undoubtedly was as startled as Jim.

Part of a panel on the back of the enclosure was missing. It was the owl's regular doorway. The offal and other debris inside showed the bird had been quite comfortable there for some time.

Permanent stands of the nailed-in kind are illegal on federal property, most likely illegal on all state property, and probably illegal on private land unless you are the landowner or have permission of the landowner to nail one in.

If you *do* put in such stands, make them large enough to draw in, and put a seat of some kind in or on it for comfort. Spray paint the wood with a dark, flat color and follow with a couple squirts of lighter toned paint. The camo job will help protect the wood and hide your stand.

I shoot left handed but have been placed in stands set up by right handers. If other people will use your stand, try to have it set up so lefties and righties can use it. They all will appreciate it. Frustration is being a lefty in a righty stand, whether that stand is permanent, portable, ground blind, waterhole pit or whatever.

Natural Stands. Natural treestands are permanent stands, of course. They range from quite comfortable to pure torture. White oak trees were made for bowhunters and for deer. Deer like to eat the acorns, and bowhunters appreciate the fact that white oaks grow strong branches at such convenient elevations and positions. These stands can be fast to get into and set up. Often a branch or branches won't be quite right—you can sit comfortably but you have to stretch your toes to reach the branch your boots will rest on, or the foot support is fine but the branch to sit on is not quite right. The woods are full of not-quite-right trees. In this instance, a wedge stand might be the answer.

Haystacks, straw stacks, windmills, abandoned buildings— they're all forms of what can only be labeled "natural" stands. If they are available in the right place, make use of them. A few judiciously placed rectangular bales can keep the wind off you, allow shooting ports like a castle tower, and be fully accepted by passing game. The second floor of an abandoned Pennsylvania

At a good sporting goods store you can examine and perhaps even test a variety of tree stands to determine which best suits your hunting requirements.

house was one of the more effective elevated stands I've seen. The house overlooked an equally-abandoned apple orchard. With the glass gone, the only problem a waiting bowhunter had was wind direction—which he solved by picking up his chair and moving it to the side of the window so he could still see the orchard but be out of the wind.

Wedge Stands. Wedge stands are small, hinged wooden platforms, light and easy to carry. Snapped into place, they can produce a comfortable perch for hours, with the shooting lanes you need. Commercial models exist, but they also are easy to make. A big double-strap barn door hinge, wood screws and a chunk of $^5/_8$-inch plywood of adequate size are all that is needed. A wedge will fit in most any daypack.

Sling Stands. Slings, which you sit in like a very short hammock, will suspend you from a branch relatively comfortably. This style of stand, or sit, lets you move around the tree fairly easily for a shot at most any angle. The toughest part of using one of these devices is becoming accustomed to the belt webbing in front of you, between the seat and the tree branch over your head. The belt also can be strapped around the trunk, so you face the trunk.

Handiest part of the sling may be the fact that you can wrap it around your waist and leave it there until you want to climb a tree. It rides easily and is out of the way.

Ladder Stands. Ladder stands are swiftly gaining popularity. More bowhunters are leery of heights than care to admit. This is nothing to be ashamed of, but it can change your hunting style a bit. The ladder stand is their solution. It is solid, comfortable *and* supported by the ground.

Typical style has sections of two-legged metal ladder with metal rungs, sections usually four feet long, which slide together to lift the platform to eight, 12 or 16 feet. The platform is strapped solidly to a tree, and a second strap midway between ground and platform takes the play out of the ladder and makes the entire unit more secure. It also makes you feel more comfortable.

The only trick to putting up a ladder stand is being sure that you lean it toward the tree at an angle which will keep it from vaulting you outward as you climb up to fasten the platform to the tree.

Some ladder stands have seats and some don't. With the ladder rungs available to hook your boots on, it would seem that a seat would be unnecessary. That setup is comfortable, but it limits your flexibility. You will do best with a seat so you can stand if needed or turn either direction to shoot.

A good ladder stand unit, taken apart, can be strapped together and carried easily on your back. These same straps will then be used to secure the stand in place. Such a package is bulky, but not particularly heavy.

Will you be more likely to leave your scent on the ladder where game can pick it up? Possibly. If you are concerned, wear gloves or put some masking scent on the ladder.

Non-climbing Portables. Non-climbing portable stands can be fastened to the tree with rope, chain or safety belt. I've seen some homemade units which fastened with a former automobile seatbelt; I always wondered about the strength of that locking device, but the fellow who made them hasn't been hospitalized so they apparently work.

Most non-climbers have folding seats as an integral part of the complete unit. The seats usually are made of aluminum tubing and canvas. The tubing which forms the forward frame of this folding seat generally creases your thighs at the best location to shut off blood circulation to your legs. To solve this problem, put a big chunk of foam cushion on the canvas or cut a piece of thick plywood to a size which fits snugly between front and back bars of the seat. The canvas won't rip when you sit on the plywood. The seat is hard but better than it was; if you want to get fancy, pad it with foam and cover it with camo fabric.

The best position for a seat is farther from the tree trunk than it usually is. Ideally, the seat would be no closer than five or six inches, so you can sit on it comfortably and use the tree as back support. When the seat is closer to the tree trunk, you have all you can do to keep from sliding forward off it, so you brace your legs. Your legs end up being very tired and knotted.

Most stands fasten with a chain anchored on one side of the stand, looped around the tree and hooked on the other side of the stand. Bare chain is noisy when putting the stand in place. Rubber coated chain is silent but can be stiff. Rope is silent, strong and easy to work with. Use what you like.

Some stands have a solid plywood platform, others have metal gridwork. Gridwork is used to reduce weight. Either can be noisy, from a boot sole slid across the surface to ice or snow crunching on it. Outdoor carpeting silences plywood nicely but adds a little weight. Gridwork usually is quieter than a solid platform because it collects less snow or ice, and since a lugged boot sole can catch in the grid there is more of a tendency to lift your feet when you move instead of sliding them.

When you're standing at the base of a tree, planning to hang a non-climbing stand somewhere higher than you can reach, you will simplify the job if you estimate beforehand where the steps will need to be fastened so you can climb the tree. Generally, steps about 180 degrees apart will permit the easiest climbing. Space them so the step above the one you are standing on is at mid-thigh level. Next step up will be at chest level. This permits easy climbing with the minimum number of steps. Those of you who are acrobats undoubtedly will place the steps much further apart, if for no other reason than to frustrate the devil out of your short-legged friends.

Climbing Portable Stands. Climbing portable stands are not the same as springboards, although some have been used as such. These stands are no tougher or easier to get into a tree with than a non-climbing stand; they are just a different attachment style and eliminate the need for steps.

Some stands are constructed so you face the tree once you are in position; most are constructed so you can face away from the tree or toward it, turning however you wish. Both work. Smooth use is simply a matter of becoming accustomed to a particular style.

Most stands have solid platforms, but others are made of a framework and heavy canvas seat, much as a lounge chair might be.

Some styles have the supporting V bar (which goes around the tree trunk) on the upper arm of the framework, with the V shaped platform base pushed against the tree to form the locking system. Other models have the V bar which goes around the tree as part of the base of the framework, with the V which pushes against the tree positioned below the platform. Either way, the stand is supposed to remain in place because of your pressure on the platform, pushing the stand "into" the tree and locking or wedging it into place.

Support arms around the tree can have a beveled forward edge to help grip the tree, or a rubber-coated arm for a friction grip, or short, fairly blunt metal spikes to punch into the bark. The V-shaped section which does not wrap around the tree may be edged in any of these styles.

Do these stands damage trees? Sharp edges on a beveled blade certainly will cut into soft, smooth bark such as found on aspens. A

Though climbing tree stands may have an edge in popularity, remember that you can't always climb with them. Always consider the conditions you'll be hunting under most often when you purchase a stand.

dulled edge still will grip but won't have as much ability to damage the bark's inner layer. Spikes can jab holes through the outer bark, which is why the spikes are kept short and fairly blunt—long enough and sharp enough to provide security, but not too long or too sharp.

For the most part, there is no damage. The bark gets scuffed, but generally that's about it.

Can these stands slip? Sure, anything is possible, but the best designs rarely, if ever, slip.

Smooth bark and bark from which small chips can pop free are the slipperiest. Get some pine bark chips caught under the support blade and the ride down may be swift.

My personal preference is the style which has the wrap-around bar on the base of the platform and the support V pushing into the tree as part of a lower unit below the platform, pushing down into the tree at about a 35-40 degree angle. No matter where you stand on this design, your weight pushes the stand into the tree, meaning that it is solid. This design is rigid, too, which means that it locks firmly in place and won't flex when you step on one side or the other. A good treestand must not rock or slip when you place your weight off center left or right.

With the framework all beneath the platform, there are no side support arms to get in the way of your bow's lower limb tip. That is a decided advantage. The only device above the platform is the seat.

Various models of the other attachment system are just as secure, I'm sure. When the support arms for the V bar which wraps around the tree are above the platform, hooking your boot toes behind these arms gives you a better sense of security and a more solid footing.

The main thing to be sure of is that the stand does not tip free easily when you stand on the back of the platform close to the tree. You should be just as secure there as at the forward edge of the platform, even though your weight will be applying much more pressure when you stand on the forward edge of the platform.

If you're going to use a climbing treestand, use a hand climber too. The climber works on the same pressure locking principle as the stand, and it makes climbing a tree much easier. Wrapping your arms around the trunk is a quick way to pull a muscle, rip your jacket, slide down the tree and tear skin loose from hands, wrists, forearms and chest.

With hand climber and treestand on the tree, put your toes under their strap on the platform and hook the other rubber strap around both heels. Push the hand climber above your head, hang from it and lift your heels. This frees the treestand. Lift your legs, then raise your toes and set the treestand in place against the trunk. Repeat this procedure until you reach the desired height. Many hand climbers are constructed so they can be used as seats when you reach the right height.

With practice, you can climb a tree silently. This will not seem possible the first few times, but keep at it.

You want the treestand platform to be slightly above horizontal when positioned at the right height. This is the most comfortable position for long-term standing. A platform that is truly horizontal will feel as if it is sloped downward slightly and will make you uncomfortable.

To achieve the desired angle, the platform will most likely be pointing higher above horizontal than desired at the base of the tree. However, as you climb and the tree trunk becomes smaller in diameter, the platform will drop to the desired angle.

Find the largest wingnuts which will work on the bolts holding the V bar around the back of the tree. One of these needs to be removed—no matter what the temperature or weather conditions—in order to slip the bar around the tree.

Frustration is defined as the effort made trying to control—and find when dropped in the leaves—a wingnut for this bar when the temperature is below freezing.

Best solution to this problem I've seen is a big knobbed device which substitutes for the wingnut. It can be gripped easily in cold weather even while you are wearing gloves.

Using a climbing stand, you will be limited to trees with diameters smaller than the span of the stand's support arms. Using a non-climber, the length of the chain or rope is your only limit to tree size.

There is no law which says climbing treestands cannot be used in branched trees, positioned and used as a non-climber. Years ago, a fellow wrote to me and asked if he could use a brand name climbing stand in a cedar tree. I wrote back and told him he could if he cut all the branches off first. This lippy response did not earn a thank you; it also was slightly inaccurate. I assumed the gentleman wanted to use the stand to climb the tree, but he may have asking simply if he could use it in the cedar. Sure he could, as a non-climber, by removing only those branches necessary to give adequate space for the stand, his body and shooting.

I must confess to preferring non-climbing stands in wet weather. Climbing a tree in wet weather is dangerous enough as it is, but the added thrill of possibly sliding down a wet tree with a stand strapped on my boots doesn't entice me.

Some treestands are camouflaged at the factory, others must be camouflaged when you take them home. Cover all the metal and top and bottom of the platform. The base color usually is dark, with light splotches to break it up. However, since the stand is part of a mottled background, you might want to try the reverse—a light or gray base color with dark splotches over it.

Climbing Steps

Steps strap on or screw into the tree. In some states screw-in steps are illegal because they may damage the tree. Screw-in steps are available as single-piece or folding units.

For easiest use, the lag screw should have a long taper. Blunt screw tips look like the nose of an earthworm and screw into hardwoods just about as easily.

A good step will point slightly upward when screwed in. This holds your boot more securely.

Safety Belts

A webbed belt with a secure locking arrangement is a necessity. The locking arrangement must also be easily unlocked or pulled free, should you slip and fall. Once your fall is broken, you can right yourself or possibly grab hold of a branch, then release the buckle. This certainly beats falling headlong to the ground.

The locking setup I prefer is simply two O rings sewn into an end loop. The other end of the belt is fed through both rings, then doubled and the looped end fed back over the inner ring and under the second. Pressure against the rings locks the belt securely, yet it can be pulled free simply by tugging on the loose end of the belt.

A single, long belt can be looped around the tree and your body, or you can use two belts, with one fastened tightly around the tree and the other fed inside that belt, then around your body and locked. The latter method keeps the belt out of your way if you need to turn to shoot back past either side of the tree.

Your safety belt can be a good place to hang a pack if no better place in the tree exists.

The belt serves an additional, and extremely useful, purpose— you can lean against it to draw and shoot. With the excitement of the shot, you may forget where you are anyway and lean or bend for the best shot angle. If both feet are firmly planted, you are extremely solid and secure.

You may want to adjust the belt according to whether you are sitting or standing. Belt webbing doesn't slide smoothly on tree bark, so just hitch it up or down when you stand or sit so the belt remains at waist level. Shorten the belt a bit when you sit, because you generally don't lean as far forward to shoot from a sitting position as you would from a standing position. The shortened belt thus will be safer.

Lift Cord

It is foolhardy and clumsy trying to climb a tree with a bow in your hand or over your shoulder. The only sensible way to get a bow into and out of a treestand is with a light cord. Duck decoy anchor cord is excellent, and since it is dyed green it is camouflaged should you leave it hanging.

Wind whatever length you need, plus a little more, onto a chunk of wood, and tie a metal snap on the loose end. All you need to do is unwind the line, hook the snap on the bowstring, make sure you have the other end secured and climb the tree. Then pull the bow up to you. When leaving a stand, lower the bow to the side so you won't fall on it if you should slip, and climb down.

Simple, easy and safe.

Bow Holder

A screw-in bow holder is an inexpensive little hook that makes life easier in the stand. Screw it into a branch, hang your bow on it and give your arm muscles a rest.

Hang the bow so it is within close, easy reach when you need it so you make as little movement as possible.

Yes, pockets sewn on pant legs will hold the bow when you rest the lower limb tip in such a pocket. Either way is good. I have pockets on all my camo pants, but I also carry a bow holder in my pack anyway. And I try like the devil not to forget it in the tree.

6

Learning
To Shoot Your Bow

Good archery is 95% mental. The mental part of archery is much greater than we often believe. The physical part is important, and the mechanical (equipment) part is important. However, the mental part controls what the physical does and thus also controls the mechanical part.

That is why it is so important to *understand* what you are doing, understand what the mind does. You won't get the best from yourself unless you *understand*, and you cannot understand unless your mind is working and *accepting* what it should accept. This applies in setting up and shooting the bow as well as in hunting efforts. When you understand and know *why* something happens, you can solve problems more quickly and easily and set up new equipment or scout and hunt a new area more quickly and easily.

We like to try to fool ourselves and blame the equipment setup when something goes wrong in our shooting. That's why one of the keys is to honestly point the finger at ourselves when a finger needs to be pointed. We cannot shy away from that; we have to make a decision. We have to admit to ourselves the good and the poor things we're doing in our shooting. After all, any bow made can shoot arrows better than we are able to make it shoot. We have to understand that we make mistakes and correct them *and* that we can put things together right. Many shooters have trouble accepting their mistakes because it focuses attention on their inner self, and that makes them uncomfortable.

Good equipment is important, but it does only what it is set up to do and what it is made to do when we release the bowstring.

Again, *good archery is 95% mental.* To do your best, you have to think positively, think all the time. You have to want to succeed, be willing to work at it, develop and keep good attitudes because they become habits. Learning to shoot the bow and arrow is easy; learning to shoot it well takes some work. Approach and solve all problems as they arise and your shooting efforts—all efforts really—will be much more rewarding and much less painful.

Just remember: Every problem actually is an opportunity for improvement.

When we begin learning to shoot the bow and arrow, and begin developing our shooting form, we must above all else remember that we are physical individuals. We have different body structures, arm lengths, neck lengths, jaw shapes, chest sizes, hand and finger sizes, etc. It is not wise to try to copy someone who shoots well, for the things which work well for that person may not work at all for us. When we begin, we cannot know right away what our best form and shooting style will be, so we must concentrate on learning the basics, experimenting until we find the things which are most comfortable, get good coaching (formal and informal) if we can, and remember at all times that it is a *learning* process.

We also must keep in mind that to learn something we had better start making mistakes. Mistakes are made only when we try to improve. We learn more from our mistakes than our successes anyway. Even a blind squirrel finds an acorn once in a while.

Two more things before getting into the basics of learning to shoot well:

1) *Learning to shoot well is not learning to put a bunch of arrows in the bullseye. Good shooting is learning to make one shot right, and then being able to duplicate that one shot time after time, from whatever position and from whatever distance planned.*

This works particularly well for the bowhunter, for it is the first shot which must count nearly all the time. Rarely is there an opportunity for a second shot.

Condition yourself to think "one perfect shot...the first shot!" You will give yourself a running start toward shooting and hunting success.

2) *When hunting, you must always work for the highest*

percentage shot. You won't always get it, but that is what you must work toward.

This means you must understand and accept that your target shooting proficiency may not translate completely to the hunting scene. You might be deadly on the target range to 70 yards, but in hunting a lot of negative things can happen between your position and a game animal 70 yards away. The animal can move; a wind can blow the arrow off course; an unseen twig may deflect your arrow. At your best hunting sites, you might not even be able to see 70 yards, or to whatever long distance you are accurate on the target range.

You must be skilled— putting all your arrows in a pieplate at 20 yards, for instance—but you must also realize the shooting distance limits which the hunting situation imposes.

You must become a good hunter as well as a good shot. That's the best combination, of course, but the next best combination is a person who is a good hunter but only an average shot, for he will be able to place himself in high percentage situations within his shooting range limits. A person who is an excellent shot but a poor hunter might not even know what his/her shooting limits should be and could end up taking low percentage shots because of an inability to get within high percentage range.

In sum, spend enough time on the shooting range, but don't spend too much time there. Shooting skills cannot make up for a lack of hunting skills. The bow is a shooting tool, not a crutch.

This shooting information is fairly detailed, for a purpose: More people quit bowhunting because of shooting and equipment tuning problems....they can't hit what they are shooting at...than for any other reason. They may blame it on lack of success, but that lack of success is caused by the underlying problems. It shouldn't be that way. Shooting can be fun, should be fun. It must be fun to be rewarding.

How to Determine Your Master Eye

Extend an arm straight in front of you. Close your fingers and stick your thumb straight up. With both eyes open, use your thumbnail as a sight and sight at a small target a short distance away.

Now close one eye, open it and close the other eye. With one of these views your thumbnail should be right on the target; with the other view your thumbnail will be to the side of the target. Your dominant or master eye is the one which shows the thumbnail

The photo on the left is what you'll see when you open your dominant eye. The right photo is the view with the subordinate eye open.

right on the target. If your thumbnail is on target with your left eye closed, you are right-eyed and should shoot right handed. If your thumbnail is on target with your right eye closed, you are left-eyed and should shoot left handed.

Very few people have equally dominant eyes, which means they could shoot whichever way they prefer. More people have a crossover than equal dominance, meaning that they are right handed but have a left dominant eye, or are left handed but have a right dominant eye. If you have this crossover condition, I assure you that it will be best to train yourself to shoot on the dominant eye side, especially if the eye is quite dominant. This will add to the beginning struggle but will pay off in ease of aiming and thus more pleasure later on. I began shooting a bow right handed, had all sorts of problems, then discovered I have a dominant left eye. It took me a couple months of clumsiness to make the switch to left handed shooting, but I am glad I did.

Building Blocks To One Perfect Shot

Assuming you have a bow you can handle, and that the arrows and bow are matched properly to you, here are the steps. These instructions are for finger shooting. You can learn how to use a release aid later, if you wish. The principles are the same.

Stance. Straddle the shooting line with an *open* stance. Your back foot will be parallel to the shooting line; your front foot will be somewhere between a 30 to 45 degree angle off a direct line to the target. Feet should be shoulder-width apart with weight distributed evenly on both feet.

This stance gives good balance and prevents normal body sway. Make a conscious effort to place your feet in the same place for every shot. Mark the positions if you wish. This is the first and very important step in developing shooting form consistency.

Nock an Arrow. Keep this part as simple as possible and with minimal movement. Use the same motion each time, for ease later on.

The nock point can be marked temporarily with adhesive tape wound several times around the string. The *bottom* of the nock should be $1/8$- to $1/4$-inch above horizontal. If you wish, use regular nock sets, one above and one below the nock for maximum security. It will keep the arrow from sliding down the string.

The nock should fit the string snugly but not too tightly. Snugness keeps the arrow from falling off the string as you draw and keeps you from releasing the string when the arrow isn't fully nocked.

The odd, or cock, feather must point at 90 degrees away from the string and away from the sight window when you are using a three-fletched arrow. The two hen feathers will lie closest to the sight window. If you are using a four-fletched arrow, it makes no difference which way you nock the arrow.

String Hand. Form a Boy Scout salute with the first three fingers of your bow hand. This positions your hand to receive the string, keeps your little finger off the string, folds your thumb against your palm and positions it at an angle which will fit under your cheekbone or jawbone at anchor.

Put the string between your index finger and your second finger, deep in the first crease of your finger joints, or just back of the first joint. Your fingers will curl around the string, forming a deep hook. This gives you a confident hold on the string and helps keep the arrow from falling off the arrow rest or shelf as you begin to draw.

Keep the back of your hand straight with your arm and relax your wrist. The tension should be only in your fingers.

Bow Hand and Bow Arm. The bow should fit in the V of your index finger and thumb, with finger and thumb forming a loose ring around the bow handle. The bow will be held against the muscle pad below your thumb. With the loose finger-thumb ring, your hand conforms well to the shape of the bow handle and will help prevent flinching or grabbing for the bow when you release.

Fingers and wrist on the bowstring will be relaxed.

Turn the bottom of your bow arm elbow away from the string and hold your elbow straight and stiff. Lock it if you can. Turning your elbow away from the string gives better string clearance, keeps the string from whacking your bow arm when you release.

Use a long armguard now; your shooting form isn't developed well enough for the shorter arm guard to adequately protect you.

Head Up, Shoulders Back. Lift your head and look at the center of the target. Bow hand, elbow and string hand are still in the position set a moment ago. This becomes the "unit." You are in a transition step which establishes a positive target attitude and unit position. While in this position you can recheck your bow hand, bow arm and string finger position.

Raise the Unit, Pre-Draw Aim. Raise your bow arm and drawing arm to shoulder level. If you are aiming without a bow sight (called "instinctive" aiming) with both eyes open (for necessary depth perception), place the tip of the arrow about 18 inches below the target center (using a 36-inch target face, 20-30 feet away). Shift your eyes to the center of the target and concentrate on the very center of the target without moving the unit. This is called "gap" aiming.

If you are aiming with a bow sight, place the end of the sight pin in the middle of the target and hold this general sight location.

The pre-draw or gap aiming method lets you aim before the stress of full draw. It puts your bow arm in the proper position with the target, gives a consistent basic aiming technique, and you won't be preoccupied with aiming as you will be at full draw. You can concentrate on your form. This is most effective at close range—20 yards or less—which is the distance you will be shooting when beginning. Actually, a big target 10 feet away is a good starting setup. Why? Psychological boost. Everyone wants to hit the target. The teachers call it "immediate participation, immediate reward."

With a sight pin, do not overemphasize the sighting procedure

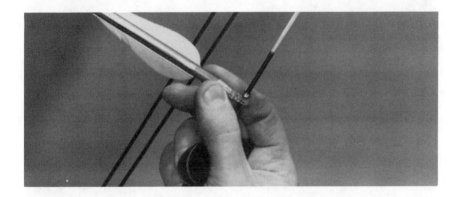

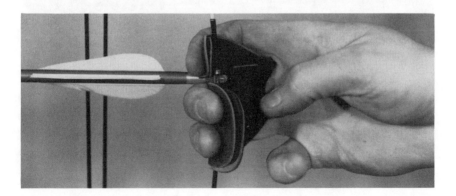

Perfect the basics of foot placement, proper nocking and proper grip and you'll have a good start to become a better bow shot.

Bow is comfortably in "V" of index finger and thumb. Fingers and wrist on string are relaxed. Turn your bowarm elbow away from the string and hold it stiff. This gives better string clearance.

Raise the unit and pre-draw aim. Without a sight, the arrow will be positioned below the target. With a sight, place the pin in the middle of the target and proceed.

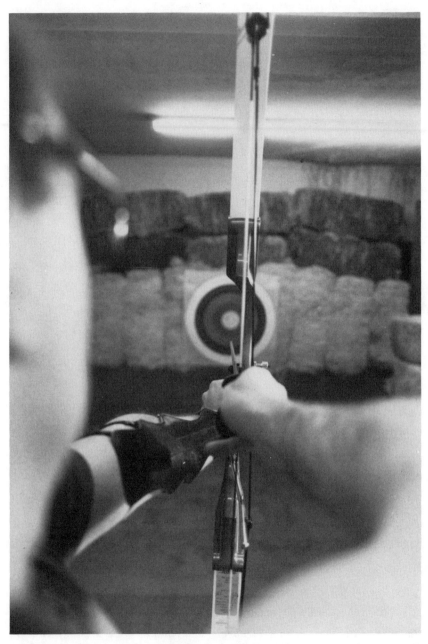

Shooter's view of pre-draw aiming without sights.

Try different anchor points until you find the one you're most comfortable with. Then stick with it!

The side anchor release and follow through. Smooth as silk.

at this learning stage or you will lose concentration on building good form.

With either style, try for arrow grouping. Aim at the bullseye consistently, but don't be concerned yet if they group somewhere off the bullseye. Grouping tells you that your equipment is performing well and that you are doing the shot sequence identically each time. That is much more important than a bullseye, because getting bullseyes once you can group arrows is no more than making an aiming adjustment.

Concentrate on the spot you intend to hit with the arrow. This helps develop your concentration powers for a smooth shot sequence and easier repetition.

Bow Arm. Overall, speaking from my experience and the experience of others, if you can develop a rock solid bow arm you will avoid or lick most of the shooting problems which can develop.

Full Draw. Hold the pre-draw aim or sight position and keep your bow arm straight, elbow locked. *Draw the string by pulling with your shoulder and back muscles.* The feeling should be of your shoulder blades pulling toward each other. Your drawing elbow should be a bit higher than your drawing shoulder.

To anchor, touch the corner of your mouth with the tip of your index finger while your thumb slides along and drops behind and under your jaw. (Options: Anchor against the bottom of your cheekbone, or under your jaw.)

Keep full draw by constant pulling from shoulder and back muscles. The high drawing elbow gives better alignment and back tension. The anchor must feel secure at all times and will feel secure if you locate it at a position that is easy to duplicate on each shot.

Your anchor thus becomes your rear sight.

Hold and Aim. Concentrate on the very center of the target and hold the sight position there. At the same time, you should have a constant feeling of tension in drawing arm, shoulder and back muscles.

Focus your eye on the target; let the sight become blurred. Line the string on the iris of your eye and look "around" the string (which will be out of focus and appear fuzzy) on both sides of the string. This insures string alignment and aiming. Your eyes concentrate on the center of the target while your mind concentrates on continuing the back tension. Hold firmly and confidently for a slow count of three to let this good image and feeling burn into your mind and muscles.

Release. With proper concentration and your anchor solidly in place, begin increasing your back tension so your shoulder blades feel like they are pulling toward each other and pulling your drawing elbow back. As this occurs, relax your string fingers. The increase in shoulder and back tension activates your string hand to relax.

The release takes place by relaxing the entire string hand from your wrist forward, and the string should feel like it is sliding in a smooth, straight line through your fingers, almost as if it is being pulled straight forward, pushing them out of the way with ease. This is a "live" release and is the best way to make certain you maintain necessary back tension and have a smooth release and follow through.

Follow Through. As your string fingers slide back along your jaw, touching the side of your neck, your bow remains in line with the target and your eyes continue concentrating on the center of the target. Hold this follow through until you hear the arrow hit thetarget. Proper eye concentration on the center of the target prevents flinching and peeking. Your shooting form doesn't fall apart with the release and follow through but remains positive and constant.

You should not see the arrow in flight. Your bow hand and the bow itself will obscure it if you do things right.

Your follow through should be a natural reaction to the increased back and shoulder tension which created the release. Follow through should not be forced or inhibited.

Make A Mental List

These steps in your shot sequence must become part of your mental checklist, to be used—consciously and subconsciously— each time you shoot an arrow. This will strengthen your form, increase your confidence and keep you from shooting too fast. Fast shooting nearly always means you have not fully, carefully and confidently prepared your form for each shot and have not aimed properly. Rushing things just doesn't work well.

Personalizing Your Form

As you learn, you probably will want to try variations on the basic form unless that form feels comfortable.

Variations can include a square or closed (also called oblique) stance, but I can tell you that neither of them allow as much clearance as the open stance, and when you are wearing added clothing, string clearance becomes more critical and difficult.

You can try high, low or straight wrist, and high or low bow shoulder.

Wrist positions vary according to whichever you feel most comfortable with and can duplicate most easily shot to shot. A low wrist most likely will be easiest for bowhunting because the pressure goes directly into your arm, whereas with a straight or high wrist you need to maintain more and consistent muscle tension in the wrist. That can be difficult with a target weight bow and extremely difficult with a hunting draw weight bow.

A high bow shoulder is pushed up and back, looking as if the muscles were tired and could not hold the shoulder lower. This can be uncomfortable after a while, and it shortens your draw length. A low shoulder takes more strength but gives better clearance and back tension. Few shooters have a classic high or low shoulder but develop whatever feels most comfortable and works best for them, and that probably is somewhere between a high and low shoulder.

Anchor Aids

Kisser Buttons. A kisser button adds a positive check for best head angle on every shot and helps control draw length, reminds you to keep your teeth together (so your jaw stays in the same elevation against your thumb at anchor with each shot) and makes you feel more confident. Don't add it until you get decent form, if you add it at all.

Peep Sights. A peep sight helps control head angle and positions your anchor finger, insures proper string alignment, helping your confidence. Work on the basics before adding it.

Shooting at close range (8-12 feet) with your eyes closed at a large, empty target butt is excellent practice to develop your shooting form. Since there is no target face to aim at, with eyes shut you concentrate solely on shooting form. Your muscles become more sensitive and your mind works with them much better.

With a target face on the butt, it is too doggone easy to forget about form development and start worrying about the bullseyes. If you develop solid form, the bullseyes will come.

The large butt and close distance are merely safety measures.

Eye Control

Good eye control helps follow through and accuracy. It is a

conscious effort to keep your eyes in alignment and focus on the target until the arrow hits. It also is tough to do in the excitement of the shot at game. Good eye control helps keep you from peeking around the string or by moving your bow arm down out of the line of vision. These bad habits louse up accuracy immediately.

7

Tuning Your Hunting Bow

There is a simple way to drive yourself crazy—make bow tuning for bowhunting unnecessarily complicated by approaching it any way other than methodically.

Our goal is to have the fastest, heaviest arrow possible which will still give *consistently* good performance.

I hesitate even using the word "fastest" because this whole business of the search for ultimate arrow speed bothers me. It's easy to put too much emphasis on speed and let other equally important or more important aspects suffer.

Lighter, faster arrows are touchier to tune and shoot. They also are less efficient, and that can create a system noise problem. A lighter arrow takes less energy from the bow than does a heavier arrow. With more energy than desired remaining in the bow's limbs, that energy can shake screws loose or cause cable noise problems when the shot is made. The stored energy at full draw has to be dissipated somewhere upon the shot, and the more energy that goes into the arrow the less there is for dissipation elsewhere in the system.

Tuning is easiest with properly matched equipment. This cannot be over-stressed. The arrow must match the peak draw weight at your draw length. If you are having a bit of a matching problem, arrows on the too-stiff side are more stable than arrows on the too-flexible/lighter side. Heavier/stiffer shafts will give better, more consistent flight in a less-than-perfect situation.

Groups Are The Key To Performance

When all your shots hit in the same spot, all you need do is change your sight setting to move them to the bull's eye. It would be nice if broadheads grouped at the same point of impact as your field points, but that is very seldom the case. Good flight and tight grouping mean the most.

We will hit the highlights here in tuning for hunting, because there is a lot to be covered. A book could be written on the subject, and it has been: *Tuning Your Compound Bow*, by Larry Wise. Some of his comments are basic, so this may be only review for you.

1) Proper Draw Length

The most important factor at the start is determining your proper draw length. This affects the arrows you get and the bow you get; you will perform poorly with an improperly fitted bow. Remember that you will shoot a shorter arrow when shooting with a release aid than with fingers, because the release simply is an extension of your fingers.

Best length is with a comfortable anchor and the bow drawn to the middle of the valley (the lowest draw weight point when the bow lets off past peak weight). Remember, too, that your hunting arrows will be longer than your target arrows, probably by an inch or more, so the broadhead will clear the sight window *and* your bow hand fingers.

2) Arrow Rest

You will have better tuning chances if you use an arrow rest that has lateral and vertical adjustments, or at least a bit of flexibility in both directions. If you apply too much downward pressure on the nock with a finger, the arrow will jump from a too-rigid rest but won't jump from a rest flexible enough to absorb that improper pressure.

Arrow rest positioning is usually referenced relative to the degree of centershot of the bow, centershot adjustment being the left-right movement of the rest or cushion plunger. Metal handles can have more centershot than wood handles, (i.e., be cut further past center), because of their inherent structural strength. Centerline reference here means the vertical center of the handle, which is the center of pressure. You cannot base the center on the limbs because their center usually doesn't match with the handle's center.

Most finger shooters have their arrow ride just outside the centerline; most release shooters set their arrow directly through the centerline.

3) Draw Weight

Check your bow's draw weight with a scale. Bows sometimes aren't set at the weight the sticker says they are. You can cause yourself big headaches if you assume the weight is what the sticker says. If you want to change the draw weight, be sure you turn the top and bottom weight bolts the same number of turns.

4) Nocking Point

Set your nocking point about one-fourth inch above level as a safe starting point. This will allow the bottom of the arrow shaft to be level to or slightly above its resting place on the arrow rest. Remember that this is only a starting point; you may need to adjust up or down the string. An arrow riding too low can give all sorts of false readings as you tune. When the nocking point is slightly too high, fewer unwanted side affects are caused.

A few wraps of adhesive tape or string make a good, temporary nocking point locator for beginning testing.

5) Shooter Consistency

Developing a consistent draw length so you always shoot from the middle of the valley at full draw is extremely important. If you draw through it to pull against the wall, which is as far as you will be able to draw, you will affect arrow matching and performance, and if you don't draw far enough you will also affect arrow matching and performance.

One big benefit of consistent draw length to the middle of the valley is that you can tune your bow to the arrow, getting a fine match without needing to buy additional arrows of different sizes.

When you shoot from the front slope ahead of the valley, arrows get a harsh start and often kick critically high. Shooting from the wall, you can get even more erratic arrows, with some arrows going high and some low.

The cam bow exaggerates these problems, compared to a round wheel compound, because the cam has steeper increases and decreases in draw weight in front of and behind the valley. The round eccentric wheel usually offers the best possible starting conditions for an arrow shot by a human.

The most important feature of the valley is the smoothness of acceleration obtained when releasing an arrow.

6) Fletch Contact

After you have done these setup steps, shoot a few arrows to check for fletch contact with the arrow rest. Spray some white foot powder on the fletchings and you will be shown quickly after each shot any contact that exists. Spray the arrow rest and sight window, too. Any contact will leave a mark.

Severe contact may mean you need to change arrow size. Lesser contact can sometimes be eliminated by rotating the nock on the arrow. Severe contact may be caused by several things: the arrow may be too stiff, the nock may be too tight on the bowstring or you may be torquing the string with your fingers at full draw. Remember that an arrow *acting* too stiff may not actually be too stiff.

Check the physical size of your rest. It may be too wide or too thick to allow clearance.

You may not be able to eliminate all contact. If that's the case, shoot feathers because they are more forgiving than vanes, giving way when contacting a rest, etc.

7) Paper Testing

Now try some paper testing. If you do paper testing, shoot through newspaper from one or two yards and go to five if you want. Right-handed shooters want a hole in the paper that is perfect or that shows the nock slightly high and left. Left-handed shooters want holes that tear perfectly or slightly nock high right.

This lift indicates the nock end of the arrow is rising slightly and will clear the arrow rest. Stay within five yards for best readings; arrows do their most bending at seven to eight yards as they try to recover in flight, and beyond the five yard distance you can get false readings.

Arrows which tear holes with the nock low are starting with the nock too low. If the hole tears too high, the nocking point is too high.

A rule of thumb is to get a hole that is no more than $^1/_2$-$^3/_4$ of an inch nock high.

Arrows that are too weak in spine will tear holes with the nock far left for a right handed shooter, far right for a left handed shooter.

Too-stiff arrows tear holes to the right for a right handed shooter and tear left for a left handed shooter.

For arrows that are too weak, reduce the draw weight or increase the tension of the cushion plunger before you try other arrow sizes. Try moving the cushion plunger in or out, probably out. This may not show much change, but sometimes it will. Tuning is totally individual; what works for you may bomb for your buddy.

For too-stiff arrows, increase the draw weight or decrease the tension of the cushion plunger.

The last resort for either condition is to try a different arrow rest.

Be patient and thorough! Test with fletched arrows. Remember that the most difficult situation to correct in tuning is that of the too-stiff arrow. Relatively good flight but inconsistent grouping is the mark of a too-stiff arrow. This can drive you crazy, because you will get a good group one time and a poor group the next time. You think the problem is in your shooting form, when it most likely isn't.

A too-weak arrow usually gives poor arrow flight and poor groups, which you will read quickly and make changes just as quickly.

8) Steering The Arrow

For shoot testing, begin at 15-20 yards. This part requires patience and repetition. If problems arise, you may need to backtrack in your tuning efforts.

With broadheads, remember that there now are "wings" on both ends of the arrow — blades and fletches. The fletches must do the steering; if blades do the steering, your arrows can strike anywhere.

The steering ability of vanes is less than that of feathers of equal size. The ribbed side of the feather creates more drag and stabilizes an arrow more quickly. Vanes don't absorb water and are quieter in the quiver. It's a trade-off decision you will have to make. If I'm hunting in weather which threatens to get pretty damp, I cover myself by putting a couple of vane-fletched arrows in my quiver to go with the feather-fletched ones I always have.

Whatever you use, be sure you have big enough fletches to control the shaft. Three fletches or four — that's personal choice. They should be attached with a helical style or straight offset at the least. This gives spin stabilization that is needed. You're asking for trouble if you glue fletches straight down the shaft and/or if you use fletches which are too small.

Blade size on the broadhead has a direct effect on arrow flight, so if the head you use has big blades, you will need plenty of fletching and ought to attach it helical style for best spin stabilization and control.

A broadhead mounted crooked on the shaft is the most difficult situation to control. Check your arrows/broadheads by spin testing each one on your thumbnail or upright on a tabletop. If it wobbles, then it needs to be straightened.

Any broadhead will uncover problems that weren't showing up when you tested with field points, so don't hesitate to change anything in your setup if you need to. Your broadheads are a different projectile and may require different tuning.

Be sure you test with all silencing devices on your bow, cables and bowstring, with arrows in the bow quiver if that's how you will shoot the bow when you are hunting. Silencing devices include moleskin on the arrow rest if needed; drawing a shaft across a bare arrow rest or over Teflon can be noisy. Basic Rule: Test broadheads one month before season so adjustments can be made if needed.

Final tuning can be a drop of Lok-Tite on screws, a lubricant on the wheels, and moleskin above and below the arrow rest to silence any accidental arrow clatter.

Be Methodical, Be Patient

Remember to be methodical and patient. Test for one thing at a time. If you try to accomplish too many things at once, you may find yourself looking for a concrete wall to bash your head against, only because it will feel so good when you stop. Remember, too, that if the logical things don't work in your tuning efforts, try something illogical. It may work, and it certainly is worth a try.

Tuning Recurve And Longbows

Recurves and longbows don't have the letoff valley to contend with during tuning, but tuning principles and efforts remain the same.

Matched equipment is still matched equipment: You *must* have the arrow's stiffness matched to your draw weight at your draw length. The problem encountered here is that many times the shooter releases the bowstring before reaching full draw. Why? Simply because there's a lot of resistance on that bowstring as you come closer to full draw, and that heavy draw weight is difficult to hold, more difficult than the reduced holding weight encountered with compound/cam bows.

Since you often release the bowstring before reaching full draw, you actually are not shooting that bow at the draw weight developed at full draw, but at some point less. This, then, can produce a mismatched arrow. How much does this happen, and to what degree? That's impossible to answer, because each of us is different.

You need to check the factory-stated draw weights at factory-stated draw lengths.

The principles of performance remain the same.

You need to develop a consistent anchor point and draw length, as would a compound bow shooter searching for the bottom of the valley.

You need to remember that your draw length with a recurve or longbow will be shorter than with a compound, simply because of the difficulty in holding the increased draw weight at full draw.

You probably won't need to rotate the nocks on your arrows as you would with a compound setup, but you never know until you check. Clearance is clearance, no matter what setup you are working with.

And you still need to be methodical in your tuning efforts.

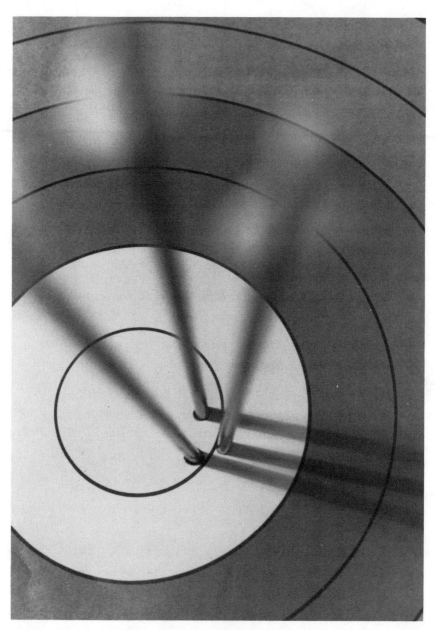

Tight groups on a traditional target butt are nice, but they become meaningless when you get one shot at a living, breathing trophy.

8

Practical Practice
For The Bowhunter

Our goal in shooting practice at this stage of skill development is to get ready for hunting. Nothing more; nothing less. Unfortunately a lot of people lose sight of—or never see—that goal and simply continue their basic target practice. There's nothing wrong with honing shooting skills/techniques, but in many instances that isn't enough, and in other instances that is too much.

Sound confusing? Let's explain it.

The classic shooting stance is fine for developing and maintaining basic shooting skills. We get the feel of our equipment. It more or less becomes part of us.

My father likes to say that aiming a rifle should feel like pointing your finger, and you should feel as confident as if you simply were pointing your finger. It's the same with a bow. The bow is an old friend. We want to feel comfortable with it. We *need* to feel confident with it. We will *know* the instant an arrow leaves the bow whether or not it's a good shot. If there's a flight problem, we will be able to analyze and correct it quickly and effortlessly.

This doesn't happen overnight. Yes, it is true that learning to shoot a bow is easy, but it's a different ballgame learning to be consistently accurate with it under all sorts of shooting positions, weather conditions, time restraints, personal tension, the game animal's tension, etc.

At the moment of truth, we need to be able to act the best way at the right time. If we haven't fully prepared, we will hesitate (mentally and/or physically), hang up and probably blow the shot...or maybe not even take the shot.

This is why experienced bowhunters know there is practice and then there is the practice hunting.

Where To Practice

For most of us, our own backyard is the best place to practice. The yard certainly is convenient. It's inexpensive. We don't need to spend travel time. It's quick (unless we get roped into mowing the lawn, but that's an occupational hazard most of us have to face anyway).

Some urban areas, however, don't allow outside bow shooting in the backyard. There are plenty of ways to solve that particular problem.

Indoor Ranges. Many archery pro shops and archery clubs have indoor ranges. They are a good place to begin practice shooting. Expect to pay a shooting fee of $1 to $4 per hour at a commercial range. Club ranges may allow non-members to shoot, but usually they restrict their facilities to club members. Sometimes they will have swap agreements with neighboring clubs. The good part of shooting at indoor ranges is that weather isn't a factor, nor is darkness.

Commercial ranges attached to pro shops have a bonus. If you're planning to buy a new hunting bow, you can try various bows on the shop's range. Trying a bow is the best evaluation. Different bows appeal to different people. Not even all bows within a particular make and model shoot alike. You might like one handle style over another. One bow may feel harsh while another feels smooth. Bow selection is, indeed, a purely personal choice. Try before you buy. You'll save aggravation, save time and get set up on the right track more quickly.

Availability, or lack of availability, of indoor shooting ranges usually is the major problem. But if there isn't one in the area, there are good alternatives.

Outside Shooting. City parks often have practice ranges administered by the recreation department.

Bowhunting clubs and field archery clubs almost always have land they own or lease, on which they set up ranges with shots of various distances and difficulties. Join a club if you can. More experienced members will share their knowledge. The only caution note I can place in here is that sometimes archers forget that what

With a little imagination, your very own backyard can offer great bow hunting practice.

works for them might not work for the next archer. So listen to the advice, try it, evaluate it, then see what works and doesn't work for you.

One enjoyable practice method is plinking, also often called "roving" in older chronicles. It's really nothing more than a glorified walk through a woods—often a midsummer walk through or near hunting territory—shooting at randomly selected targets. Hunting partners can spend an enjoyable day or an afternoon and get in some good practice at the same time.

Shooting at a grass clump here, a rotten stump there, a dirt clod next, and then a sand bank. For this type of shooting, Judo Points are ideal. They prevent lost arrows and long search times because the wire prongs stop the arrow quickly. I like to take a bow along when I'm hunting morel mushrooms in the spring. The bow feels warm in my hand, and the warm season starts out right. As you can imagine, when a group of friends head out on a jaunt like this, sidebets have been known to be placed and considerable joshing usually keeps things loose.

When shooting like this, it works best to keep targets at the same elevation as the target you'll be shooting at during hunting season. For instance, for shooting at whitetails, pick a target at the same height as the heart/lung region of a deer. There's nothing scientific here, but when you shoot high you quickly learn how far an arrow can go past the intended target and why it sometimes is difficult to find an arrow that flew over the back of the real thing.

This type of shooting also is excellent distance judging practice. If you limit yourself to one arrow per target—and you should, because that's usually all you get at a particular game animal—you have excellent mental conditioning toward making that first shot count.

Now let's go back to the most likely shooting practice area—the backyard. If all that can be set up is a practice butt or 3D target, so be it. Practice is better, though, and more fun when we can add a treestand or simulated treestand, or when we have a small sandpit to shoot broadheads into. A foam target is excellent for broadhead practice. Foam targets have the added benefit of being transportable. They can be moved around the yard or tossed into a vehicle for use at hunting camp.

I've even seen a couple of backyards with the right setup for running deer targets. Two posts, two pulleys and a long loop of clothesline or heavy twine constituted the working parts. Animal targets are hung on the line. The line is pulled by someone positioned safely away from the impact area. Even though you won't get that many shots at running game, this still is enjoyable practice. When needed, the experience is good to have.

A former neighbor almost ran into a tree with his riding lawnmower the first time he saw me practicing from the roof of my garage. The guy isn't a hunter, so the sight was more than just a novelty to him. He was totally nonplussed.

I've moved to a different house, which has a small grove of cedar trees beside it. Two of those trees now have permanent treestands in them. I can shoot up to 21 yards from one and up to 45 yards from another.

For pronghorn hunting, practice shooting from a pit. Bowhunting pits dug near waterholes are excellent blinds and widely used. However, you might get a claustrophobic feeling the first time you try one. You sit on a bench dug as part of the pit and shoot just over the lip of the piled-up dirt surrounding the pit. I hunted Colorado pronghorns a few years ago with a guy who swore that he was going to sink a bathtub in his lawn and practice from it before his next pronghorn hunt. He had more difficulty than most bowhunters adjusting to pit shooting.

When's the best time to begin practice? Now. If not now, as soon as you can. *Don't wait until a couple of weeks before season*! You won't give yourself enough time to get all equipment set up and tuned, get your muscle memory built up, your confidence level built up.

How To Practice

Bowhunting shots seldom offer the classic stance, aim, release posture. You'll get shots over tree branches, under tree branches, around brush clumps, to your left, to your right, straight ahead, behind you, up, down, standing, sitting, on one leg, with one foot asleep, with a branch bumping your elbow, leaning around a tree trunk—just about any position imaginable...*and some that aren't imaginable*!

There's also the shot at game with an obstruction halfway between you and it. You'll need to know your arrow's trajectory, because the sight picture may look like you'll be trying to shoot through the edge of a fallen log while the arrow's trajectory will let it clear the log and drop right on to the money. You probably won't even see the hit, but it will be a good one.

The variabilities are endless. We can't anticipate and prepare for all of them, naturally, but we can take practice as far as time and imagination allow.

Practice while seated on a stool, seated on the ground, kneeling and standing. Use the trees, bushes and buildings in your yard as obstacles.

Practice shooting through the tops of weeds and grass. Why? Because for some psychological reason, that vegetation presents a mental barrier. We think we're concentrating on the vital area of a target half hidden in grass, but when we release the string the arrow zips right over the tops of the grass and either over the target or hits the target too high. I've tried this little trick on too many people, and seen almost all of them shoot high—even when they thought they were deeply concentrating—to chalk it up to accident or coincidence.

A friend of mine hangs his hunting bow in his garage, just inside the door. Each morning, as he leaves for work, he takes one shot at a target, retrieves the arrow and goes to work.

"One shot is what I'll get at game, so I want to practice—mentally and physically—the same way," he explains.

Darrell Pace, the only two-time Olympic gold medalist in archery, told me that he likes to practice at long range. That's 90 meters for him. (I have difficulty even seeing targets that far away.) He says the longer distances force him to aim more precisely and concentrate harder.

He also says that any distance less than 90 meters then seems easier. He doesn't slacken his aiming or concentration on shorter distances, he just has more confidence that he's going to do better on them. And he does.

I've tried this, and it works for me. I can't say whether it will work for you or whether you will like it. The main problem—other than spending extra time looking for arrows the first few times you try the long range—is the temptation to slacken our concentration or aiming on shorter shots, or to regard the shot as a "gimme" and rush it.

This practice is the time to break in new hunting gear—new bow, new arrow, new broadheads, new sight, new tab, new quiver, new hunting clothes, new boots. Boots? Better to break them in while walking from target to shooting line than on a hunt.

This is the time to check for fletching clearance, to be surethere's no noise of a feather scraping over a compound bow cable, for instance. This also is the time to be sure all your arrows are matched to you and your bow.

If you'll be bear hunting when and where mosquitoes and black flies will be a problem, practice with a headnet and gloves. You'll

Realistic situations, like shooting between trees, are not difficult to duplicate, even at home.

In your mind go through the progression of a normal days hunting, then practice all the possible shots you might get.

Practice with the equipment in place that you'll be using in the field. A string tracker can change the flight characteristics of your rig.

The practice range is the place to test out gear and clothing. Work out the bugs before you go into the field.

then be accustomed to them on the actual hunt and will be able to concentrate on aiming at the game animal.

Practice in windy weather and wet weather, because sooner or later you'll hunt under those conditions. Winds can blow an arrow off target. How far? Depends on the wind; depends on the arrow. Wet weather can produce an unwanted crease in a finger tab or shooting glove that will cause the string to hang up and give you a sloppy release. Wet weather also can affect feather fletching if you haven't sprayed the fletches with protection such as dry-fly dope.

Unwanted noise can keep you from getting a shot at game or give you a poor shot at an unnecessarily spooked animal. So make sure your gear is silent in practice. Check quiver and sight attachments for tightness. A bit of Loctite will keep them from working loose.

Maybe a rubber pad between quiver and bow will be needed.

Limb bases sometimes make a light pop as you draw the bow; you may need to tighten the mounting bolt or do something else to prevent that.

Metal arrow rests can sing like a violin when a metal arrow is drawn over them; apply a plastic sleeve or a bit of moleskin for the arrow to slide silently across. The side plate and/or cushion plunger might also need moleskin.

Rubber clips on the lower unit of your quiver may not hold arrows securely, allowing the arrows to work loose and rattle in the quiver head.

Maybe your quiver won't permit adequate spacing among arrow fletchings and they rattle against each other when you shoot, or an arrow on the inside of the quiver gets in the way of the lower limb when you release.

It's impossible to cover all the points of necessary silencing, but you get the idea.

I mentioned clothing earlier. New camo clothes can be stiff and noisy. A washing should take care of that. If the fit isn't right, a jacket may bind as you raise your arms or as you draw. The practice range is the best place to find out.

Fred Bear mentioned once that "Clothes that seem quiet when you roll the material between your fingertips in a store, or brush your hand against it, may be noisy as the devil in the woods."

He's absolutely correct. Some materials just aren't right for bowhunting. Silent clothing is important. A soft-surfaced garment that also is tough is invaluable. *Find out on the practice range!*

Shoot Your Broadheads

What's the major mistake bowhunters make when practicing for hunting? Failing to practice with the broadheads they will be shooting while hunting. Field points are excellent to begin with, but before the season opens you must switch over to broadheads and do your final tuning with them. Some brands have practice broadheads made of plastic. They're good, but I still prefer the real thing. If you're using replaceable blade heads, sacrifice a couple of them for the ultimate benefit.

Field points usually fly differently from broadheads. Both may group well, but they probably won't group in the same place. As long as the broadheads are grouping, all you need to do is adjust your sight pins (assuming you're using a bowsight) or practice enough to know what they'll do if you're shooting instinctively.

Shoot every hunting arrow you'll carry in your quiver. One arrow may have a nock glued crooked, or a shaft may be slightly crooked or cracked. You sure don't want to find that out by shooting such an arrow at a game animal. The results might turn the air blue with editorial comments.

Practice on targets of the right size of the animal you intend to hunt, and at the distances you intend to shoot. Many bowhunters don't shoot beyond, say, 25 yards at a deer. A Colorado friend of mine made a good comment on that one time. He said, "An elk is much more than twice as big as a deer, so a 50-yard shot at an elk really isn't any different from a 25-yard shot at a deer. You're shooting at a much larger vital area. If you get a good shot at an elk at 50 yards, take it. You've already got the skills to make it good."

But can you accurately judge the distance on an elk if you're accustomed to seeing and shooting at animals the size of a whitetail? That will be a problem if you haven't practiced it, and that's the value of a target the same size as the intended quarry.

When you practice from a treestand, practice all distances *and* the straight down shot. It's not an easy shot. Shots like this, and other extremely close shots, might require a different, higher anchor point. I anchor at the corner of my mouth with my index finger, but on extremely close and straight down shots I switch to three-fingers-under and gunbarrel aim. There's no trajectory to worry about, and I like to be looking right down my arrow on such shots.

Instinctive shooters often have the most problems with extremely close shots because the gap between the tip of their arrow and the target is so large. The arrow looks like it is pointing at the animal's feet or lower, and that can mess up your mind if you're not fully accustomed to it.

Practicing on animal cutouts or three dimensional targets also helps you concentrate on the heart/lung area. That area isn't marked on game animals, so you'll do better if you practice with an unmarked target. You want to do everything you can to groove your sight picture, your shooting form—and your mental image of the target. You want to become a machine or as near to it as possible. If you have to stop and think at the moment of truth, you're going to blow the shot.

Keep It Fun

All this practice can become tedious now and then, so liven it up with a couple of games.

The same neighbor who marveled at me shooting from my garage roof didn't quite know how to react the first time he saw me on the roof with my bow and a couple dozen arrows, my wife standing under the roof's overhand tossing plastic one-gallon milk jugs, me shooting at them and our kids retrieving them.

One shot per milk jug. Distance unknown. Shot angle and pose unknown. Great fun. The jug is roughly the size of the heart/lung area of a deer, and each hit makes a satisfying whack.

A handful or two of sand in the jug, with the cap screwed on tight so the sand can't fly out, lets the person doing the throwing get more distance.

Inflated balloons with a cup of water in them skitter across a lawn in irregular patterns. They're interesting targets, too.

Practice games are limited only by your imagination.

I like to reward myself on good shots by saying aloud— because it has a more positive effect than when just mentally stated—"Dead animal." I didn't realize the effect this had until my son, who was four or five years old at the time, whacked a fly with a flyswatter and pronounced, in a satisfied tone, "Dead animal." That required an explanation to my wife, because she hadn't heard my reward system but happened to be watching my son when he mashed that fly.

Too Much Of A Good Thing

I mentioned at the beginning of this chapter that honing your shooting skills sometimes can be too much of a good thing. The reason is that some bowhunters spend too much time practicing and too little time in the woods learning the terrain and the game. They forget the hunting part.

Shoot your broadheads at lifelike targets for at least a month before the season opens. Details like this spell the difference between failure and success.

Ideally, we want an excellent shot at an unalarmed animal. That's a high percentage shot. However, a person who is deadly to 70 yards on the practice range might not be able to get within good shot range. He might think anything within 70 yards is fair game, but that just isn't the way it works.

In the field, many other factors enter the picture. A vagrant breeze may blow a bit of scent toward the animal and make it suspicious, tense, extremely alert and ready to disappear. Or an unseen twig might be in the arrow's path. Or the animal may move just as you release. The possibilities for things to go wrong are seemingly endless.

Because of this, we need to know what are and are not high-percentage shots. A 20-yard shot may be duck soup on the practice range but a poor shot, because of circumstances, in the woods. Every shot is different, because conditions are different. So...know your skill level, but *also* know the percentages. The most consistently successful bowhunters are good shooters *and* good hunters.

A few years ago, a long-time bowhunter took a young and

highly skilled target archer bowhunting. The young guy really hadn't hunted before, even though he'd been in the woods a couple of times trying. He could shoot gnats at 70 yards and more, so when a deer stepped out of the brush across the small field from where he sat, he felt the 50-yard shot would be easy.

It wasn't, because the target was 55 yards away instead of 50 and it moved just as he released the arrow.

The young guy almost suffered cardiac arrest. He wasn't accustomed to unmarked distances, nor was he accustomed to targets which moved and refused to play fair.

9

The Importance
Of Anatomy/Aiming

Now let's add an important element to practice and to each actual hunt—knowing the game animal's anatomy and where to aim under various types of shots that are offered. You don't need to become a physiologist, but a good bit of anatomical knowledge is important.

For instance, a nice, fat, unalarmed deer moves past you at 20 yards. It is quartering away. You are deadly at 20 yards, so you aim just behind the shoulder and low and release the bowstring. The arrow darts forward and hits low, just behind the shoulder.

The deer races away, acting like it has been badly spooked.

Did your arrow get into the heart/lung boiler room, or did it range too far forward, missing the vital area and cutting only muscles? You won't know until you begin trailing it, and until then you will have some anxious moments.

Another instance could be a shot which strikes too far back. Did you catch the kidneys or liver? Or maybe the big artery just under the spine? Or could you have unzipped the belly cavity close to the bottom? Knowing the possibilities will give you a running start, so to speak, on knowing how and when to trail the animal.

Murphy's Law often applies when you are under the self-imposed tension of a shot at a game animal. As a friend says, "My draw length is 30 inches when I'm shooting at targets, 31 inches when I'm shooting at a doe, 32 inches when I'm shooting at an ordinary buck....and 33 inches or more if it is a big-racked buck.'' He's exaggerating, of course, but he's also saying he is susceptible to the very human tendency to get excited and overlook some of the detail at the peak of excitement and tension.

Another friend, with many years of bowhunting experience, said he and several of his equally-experienced cronies once decided to test themselves and their powers of observation under stress. On a certain day, each took a small tape recorder along to his hunting stand. Each was to record his impressions right after shooting at a deer and hitting it—exactly where it was when hit, where the arrow hit it, how far they estimated the deer would go, where and how soon they expected to find it.

''We were somewhere between surprised and shocked when we compared our tape recorded impressions and the actual situations,'' he said. ''We each had taken plenty of game with the bow, but that didn't guarantee outstanding accuracy in our observations. Some of our expert observations became humble opinions when the animals were recovered. A couple of observations were more than a foot off in estimating where the arrow had hit the animal. And since you want to say 'I *know* I hit it right where I aimed' or 'It looked like the arrow hit about four inches to the left of my aiming spot,' when you see blood sign which indicates otherwise, or movement which indicates other-wise, you have to adjust your thinking—sometimes difficult to do—and go with the signs right in front of you on the grass, leaves, brush and ground.''

As you can see, knowing the location of skeletal structure, vital organs, veins and arteries does several good things: 1) *Helps you know exactly where to aim under various shot angles*; 2) *May give you more shot opportunities*; 3) *Goes a long way toward helping you do a better job of tracking and trailing a hit animal*.

Pick A Spot

This simple instruction is vitally important, yet so difficult to follow at times. It isn't easy to pick a spot when the game animal standing before you is wearing a set of antlers or horns that ought to have outriggers just to help the animal hold up that adornment.

Sometimes it isn't easy to pick a spot if that animal is a yearling doe. It is still a wild thing that we have hunted, and the excitement of the situation carries our concentration away in a mad rush.

Just what, exactly, is meant by *pick a spot*? Concentrate your

Knowing when to take the shot and where to put the arrow are crucial to taking down trophies in short order.

mind, focus your eyes and intentions on the smallest aiming point you can on the intended target. If this means you pick out one hair and focus on it, fine. Whatever works for you, go with.

Avoid:

"Ohmigoshthere'sabuckinrange. I'mgonnashoot."

"Look at those antlers! Pick a spot. Would you look at those antlers? Pick a spot. Would you look at those...." (Guess where the arrow went? No second guess should be needed.)

"That one approaching is worth taking. I wonder if I got the squeak out of the wheel? I wonder if my clothes are too noisy? I wonder if my camo is good enough? I wonder if it will see me draw? I wonder if I'll keep cool? I wonder...what my name is? *Shoot*! (Not much doubt on where this shot will end up either.)

These scenarios are endless in variety, but they all have two things in common: a missed shot and a frustrated bowhunter.

Failure to pick a spot to put your arrow could be attributed to buck fever, but that isn't really it. Failure to pick a properly small spot is caused more by the bowhunter's looking at the entire animal. It is similar to a wide angle view, when there should be a mental zoom lens view, boring right in on that precise place you want to place your arrow.

The best way to pick a spot when the chips are down is to practice picking a spot. Remove the white paper pieplate from your cardboard target. Draw in the shoulder and foreleg outline, but don't define it brilliantly. No animal in heavy shadow or gray light has its parts brilliantly defined. Learn to focus on one tiny aspect in the proper aiming region. Don't think "heart/lungs"; think more precisely than that.

If you practice on a round target matt covered with burlap, don't use a target. Instead, select small items on the burlap and aim at them.

Do the same with any target.

You're simply grooving your mental image, your subconscious and conscious control, your muscle memory, to do everything right when tension is highest and margin for error lowest.

Pick the spot, then release at the right moment.

A Game Of Inches

Bowhunting is a game of inches. Just a couple of inches can mean the difference between a hit or miss, a fatally wounded or a superficially wounded animal.

Doing everything right under tense conditions is tough, and

Pick Your Spot!

Throughout this chapter, you'll see photos of big game animals in various situations and positions. Think about the spot you would pick to shoot at if you were presented each shot. Remember, don't pick a general area—pick a precise spot on the animal!

At the end of the chapter, you'll see the photos again marked with the author's shot choices. See how yours compare and go back to the text to see why the author picked the the spots he did.

since we're already dealing with a limited-range hunting tool, shooting a projectile in more of an arc than we think, we have to deal in inches. We can't talk "minute-of-angle" like riflemen do.

A broadhead almost always does its work by cutting; rarely is shock, such as from bone damage, involved. This work can be accomplished much more quickly and easily when you know big game anatomy and where best to aim.

We're all familiar with the quiz often given in hunter education classes. The instructor posts the outline of a deer and asks students to mark where they believe the heart is located. The positions noted are, fortunately, almost always in the front half of the body and inside the rib cage, but beyond that guesses at the exact location are pretty haphazard.

The rifle hunter is in for a shock when he takes up bowhunting; especially the guy who has learned to take neck or head shots only to avoid the animal running 100 yards and being claimed by another hunter. He fully expects a mortally wounded animal to topple over when hit. That guy's chin is going to hit the ground when he learns the whys and wherefores of good arrow placement and/or when he solidly hits his first big game animal in the heart/lung region and it takes off acting untouched.

In the bow tuning chapter we talked of the necessity of shooting the *fastest, heaviest arrow*. That's because kinetic energy is the most important factor in determining arrow penetration. Neither arrow speed alone nor mass weight alone determines penetration. Results of some studies I made from broadheads shot at the Wisconsin Bowhunters Association annual autumn shoot showed that the addition of a few grains of mass weight often improved kinetic energy more than the addition of a few feet per second in arrow speed.

The farther an arrow penetrates, the more cutting it does and more hemorrhaging it causes. The deeper the arrow goes, the more chance it has to contact vital organs and do them damage.

The fact that there is little shock can produce surprising results. Bob Barrie, who manufactures the Rocky Mountain Razor broadhead, has shot more than one deer which jumped as if stung by a bee when it was hit by the arrow, then walked over to sniff the arrow sticking in the ground after passing completely through its lung cavity, and then fell dead. That happens only on windy days when there is enough natural noise to cover the sound of the shot, and the arrow must pass through without striking bone...but it does happen, and it is not a strikingly rare occurrence.

A sharp broadhead helps reduce the potential for shock as well as getting better penetration.

Shock triggers two defense mechanisms in an animal. Noise, such as from a firearm, and sudden movement can frighten the animal into flight. Shock from bones being struck can cause physical pain, which also will frighten the animal into flight. Adrenalin is released into the blood, and the animal gets the effects of a booster rocket.

This is why a mortally wounded animal often can and does go a long way while it literally is dead on its feet. This also explains why, sometimes, a seemingly impotent hunting tool such as a bow and arrow can bring down a big animal as easily or more easily than a powerful firearm——the animal doesn't know how hard it is hit.

Here's another example which may seem unusual but isn't. On a recent Missouri whitetail hunt, I had a 21-yard shot at a yearling whitetail on the last day of the hunt. Since I had an empty freezer at home and it was the only shot I was offered, I took it. I probably shot a bit high anyway, but I also had misjudged the distance for 25 yards (not having checked it earlier with my rangefinder), so my arrow hit the deer high, in the lung cavity but under the spine. The deer took off and as far as I know is still doing fine. We followed it until the blood trail ran out.

Why? Because that location is often known as no man's land or no tag land. It is above the lungs and below the spine. The arrow punches entrance and exit holes, and that's about it. It is a superficial wound which looks, from the sight of the arrow disappearing into the animal, quite deadly.

Lungs *do not* fill their cavity ahead of the diaphragm. They cannot, because if they did they wouldn't have space to expand and contract for breathing.

A Colorado friend once hit a bull elk just above the hock with a razor-sharp broadhead. That bull was slowed down because his tendon was cut, and it left an intermittent but basically continuous blood trail. It took several hours of hard trailing, but my friend got that bull. The sharp broadhead created the necessary cut but didn't send any alarm signals to the elk's internal defense mechanisms.

The most desirable shot—no matter what the species—is at an unalarmed animal quartering away, with its near foreleg forward to expose the heart. When an animal offers this shot, your eyebrows tend to shoot up under your hatband and you keep from smiling only because this would change your anchor point.

The heart/lung region of a big game animal is the largest target and one which, when its functions are disrupted, can bring down the animal swiftly. This region is relatively unprotected, especially from the shot angle just mentioned.

Big game animals are similar in body configuration, yet there are differences worth knowing and paying attention to. A pronghorn or deer, for instance, won't have the hide or skeletal protection an elk or moose will. Bears have an underlayer of hair that is first cousin to steel wool and long outer hairs which absorb a lot of blood, meaning that you had better have a strong, sharp broadhead and get a good hit or you might have an impossible tracking job. The amount of fat on an animal affects things too, being able to plug a hole and prevent a good blood trail.

A heavy draw weight bow with a heavy arrow might smash through the shoulder blade of a smaller big game animal, but you had better not try it on a moose or bear. Deer ribs are wider and flatter than bear ribs, which look in cross section much like a half moon; there is more space to slip an arrow between bear ribs, but if you hit a rib squarely you may not get good results. Flatter, thinner ribs, naturally, are more easily penetrated.

There's also an indeterminate condition which can only be described as "the will to live." It has nothing to do with animal size and doesn't appear to have anything to do with ferocity, i.e., bears. For instance, a hard-hit bear will generally go down more quickly than a hard-hit deer, but the reverse is usually true on poor hits.

The whitetail deer is among the highest in the "will to live" department. At the bottom? "Moose," says Fred Bear. "I shot one which walked about 20 yards after the hit, leaned against an aspen sapling and went into a slow-motion topple. It leaned and leaned, the sapling bent and bent until it could bend no further and snapped off. That's when the moose fell over. It never moved from the spot. One of the darnedest things I ever saw."

Shots From Above

Bone structure and your shooting location (treestand or ground level, uphill or downhill) are prime factors in determining where to aim and whether or not a shot opportunity exists.

An animal's body generally is deeper than it is wide. Bone protection is less on the lower half of the body than the top half. Heart, lungs and liver all lie low in the body, relatively unprotected from low-angle shots.

Before we began using treestands so extensively, recurve bows of 40 to 55 pounds draw weight killed a lot of big game. Shooting from ground blinds, we were putting arrows through the narrowest axis of the animal's body *and* through the least-protected part. Complete penetration was often achieved, and even if it wasn't, the entry hole was low enough on the body that a good blood trail usually existed on a hit in the right area.

The situation changes when we climb into a treestand. We're shooting downward through the body depth, which is more than body width, at a narrower target, and we're contending with increased physical protection provided by the spinal column, wide and heavy rib bases, back and shoulder muscles, the wide upper part of the shoulder blade.

We also need complete penetration (entry and exit holes) more now than before. Assume an animal is hit in the lungs, but the arrow does not penetrate fully. That animal's lung cavity must fill with blood before it can spill out the entry hole on top, dribble down over body hair and fall to the ground. A mortally wounded animal can go a long way before beginning to leave a blood trail. That increases the chances of it becoming a lost animal.

The macho idea of a heavy draw weight bow has its own allure for some bowhunters, but the main impetus for heavier bow draw weights was the increased use of the treestand, coupled with the development of the compound bow (which made shooting heavier draw weights easier).

There's another factor, too: Ignorance. A lot of today's bowhunters, who never hunted with a recurve, have a difficult time believing that a 45-, 50- or 55-pound recurve can kill an animal. Still, I keep coming back to a fellow I know who had bypass surgery—five bypasses, to be exact—who worked up to a 32-pound bow by opening day of deer season. Hunting from a ground blind and picking his shot, he shot *clear through* a nice-sized doe that fall—with a 32-pound bow! He knew his limitations, but he also knew what the equipment could do.

When using a treestand, remember, too, that the higher you go in the tree, the poorer your shot angle and the less familiar you are with judging distances from that view. Up there in ''Nosebleed Heaven,'' where the geese flying by pass below you and your tree swaying in the wind can make you seasick, you have put yourself in a position that forces you to put an arrow through an animal's best physical protection to reach the heart/lungs. You might feel good about being well hidden and your scent out of the way at such

heights, but don't ignore the negatives.

One of the main problems encountered with increasing stand height is that the severe shot angle makes it difficult for a broadhead to catch both lungs. An animal with only one lung damaged can go a long way. I cannot overemphasize this factor. It is very important and one of the main reasons I prefer not going more than 12 feet off the ground with my treestand *and* keeping it reasonably far back from the trail, 15-20 yards or a bit more if possible and practical.

Front To Back

Before looking at various shot angles and shot opportunities, remember one other basic guideline: *the point of entry must be adjusted forward or backward as needed* when an animal is quartering, and must be *adjusted up or down* depending upon your position relative to horizontal with the animal. *Be certain the arrow's path will take it through the vitals.*

The reason there is a problem, and the necessity for emphasis here, is that we do almost all our practicing at a broadside target. We get so accustomed to that visual cue that we forget to adjust our arrow's intended point of entry when the actual animal isn't in that position.

Broadside, we put our arrows in four to six inches above the bottom line and a couple of inches behind the 'elbow' of the animal's front leg. We know that will take out both lungs, and that we have an acceptable margin for error.

Visualize a game animal quartering away from you. Now visualize the intended arrow path to and through that animal's heart/lungs region.

If we keep our intended point of entry the same as it was for a broadside shot, the arrow probably will pass ahead of the lung and cut only muscle. It might not even enter the ribcage. We must adjust point of entry backward so the arrow will range forward, into and through the lung cavity. How far back the adjustment is made depends upon how sharply the animal is quartering away.

Likewise, with an animal quartering toward us—a much less desirable shot because the animal has more chance of seeing us move and its vital areas are better protected—we must adjust the point of entry forward. Do we go behind or ahead of the foreleg? Do we go for the top of the shoulder and hope to cut the spinal column? Do we go for the juncture of neck and shoulder, hoping to get the arrow past the shoulder blade and through the ribs?

A simple training method is to visualize the desired position of the *exit hole* on the far side of the animal, then see where the desired point of entry lies on a straight line from your eye to that intended exit hole. The first couple of times you try this, you might be amazed at the number of inches the entry point needs to be moved back.

Adjust For Height

Why do we miss high so often when shooting from a treestand?

The usual reason is our unfamiliarity of judging distances from that position, plus our unfamiliarity of looking at a game animal's body configuration from that angle. We're accustomed to judging distance using a broadside, ground level view. That body depth is our major visual cue.

From the elevated position, as we look more at body width than depth and see a narrower picture, our mental training and experience tell us "Since it looks smaller, it has to be farther away. So I'll have to aim a little higher."

The problem is compounded because now the actual back and spinal column of the animal are not at the top of the sight picture; they have moved down, so to speak, more into the middle of our view of the animal, because we can see the top of the back on the off-side. We're getting more of a 3D view than a profile, and the dimension is unfamiliar.

So even if we compensate short on our distance judging, anticipating that the distance might not be as far as we think it is, we still can get a poor, high hit on that animal due to our failure mentally to adjust to a different view of the animal's bone structure, related positions of internal organs and proper point of entry for our arrow.

If we are shooting a recurve, there may be another reason for high shots. We may heel the bow and put too much pressure on the lower limb, which makes it store more energy than the upper limb and thus kick the arrow high upon release.

The reason a recurve often is unfairly blamed for penetration problems when shot from a treestand is that we often drop our bow arm instead of bending at the waist to aim and release. When we stand mostly upright and drop our bow arm, we shorten our draw length. With a recurve, this means less energy is stored in the limbs at full draw, and there is less energy available to drive the arrow. The bow gets blamed when our shooting form is the culprit.

I shot a deer in Michigan a while back which illustrated a couple of potential problems, even though things worked out fine. The deer was only about 10 yards from my treestand, which was 12 to 14 feet in the air, so the angle was a bit sharp. The animal was quartering away with its head down, feeding.

My peep sight has a fairly large diameter and I like it because it keeps me from peeking as I release, but at the time I hadn't shot it enough at game to be completely comfortable with it. At full draw, the peep sight was filled with deer hair, and for an instant I wasn't sure what part of the deer I was aiming at. But at 10 yards it couldn't be too far wrong. At the release, there was a sound of something being sliced while under tension, then the chink of blade on bone. Point of entry was right beside the spine, with the arrow glancing off it and forward to hit the upper part of both lungs. The deer went only 40 yards and sprayed blood everywhere, but the arrow could have glanced less favorably. Also, striking the heavy bone took enough energy out of the arrow that I didn't get full penetration.

Shots You May Get

Let's look at some shots:

Neck. Low percentage shot, with only the spine and the carotid arteries as legitimate targets. Spine is positioned lower, vertically, in the neck than often thought. We want to picture it near the top, but it is in the middle, and below the midline near the body.

Heart. Lower half of the heart/lung cavity, far forward. Protected by leg bone from side, shoulder blade and rib bases from above. Partially protected by ribs from side. Protected fairly well by ribs in front. Not quite flat against floor of cavity, but more cupped by lungs and off floor a bit. Massive amount of blood vessels at top of heart, which essentially adds to target area.

With a quartering-away shot, entry point will be at back of ribs and halfway down the body, from treestand view. From ground level, entry point obviously must be lower. From straight overhead, not a good target; you will either attempt to break the spine from that angle or aim to one side of the spine and attempt to catch a lung.

With a front-quartering shot, aim high on the juncture of the neck and shoulder if you are in a treestand. From ground level, aim just in front of the shoulder blade and appropriately low on the body. From straight in front, this isn't a good target unless the animal has its head down and you can stick it like a toreador sticks a bull in the ring. Even then, you will most likely get more lung than heart.

Lungs. Largest single target on an animal. Not as well protected as the heart. Estimate best target is lower two-thirds of heart/lung cavity. This gives most left/right latitude. Diaphragm attaches near end ribs; generally figure that the ribs cover the lungs. If you're low and too far back, you should then get the liver, which is a quickly-fatal shot.

Quartering-away shot same as heart. Quartering-toward shot can either go just behind leg bone and low, or just ahead of shoulder blade, or if you feel you have a heavy enough draw weight bow, right through the upper part of the shoulder blade. Frontal shot noted in comments on heart shot.

On any animal, aim so the arrow penetrates the lower half of the body in this area and you will have the best target.

Sometimes I wonder whether I'm imagining things, but it seems to me that a black bear's lungs extend farther back, comparatively speaking, than they do on a deer. I know a bear isn't supposed to have much lung capacity, some say roughly the size of a football for lungs and heart area. I haven't asked a bear, and by the time I'm ready to approach the ones I've shot, all the air is gone and they are in no condition to answer anyway. But I've talked with other hunters who also have shot bears farther back than they intended but ended up with lung hits.

Liver. On bottom of paunch, just behind diaphragm. Target nearly as large as lungs and with a good hit almost as quickly fatal. A sharply quartering-forward shot may pass through the liver if the angle is low enough or the shot is too far back to catch the lungs.

A few years ago, Larry Bauman, a Missouri bowhunting friend, took a huge black bear on an Ontario hunt with me. Larry's three-bladed broadhead punched a big hole in the skin high on the back and behind the diaphragm, farther back than he intended. The broadhead stopped with two blades positioned flat against the bear's liver but without puncturing it.

Though a spring bear, it had plenty of fat. The fat and the heavy hair covering and thick skin prevented complete penetration. When hit, the bear took off just as fast as you would expect it to. It ran about one-quarter mile and in the run committed suicide. As it ran, each of the two blades next to the liver slashed the liver to ribbons.

Kidneys. Small target high in mid-range of paunch/intestinal cavity. Good hit, but almost always by accident. Large artery to rear quarters in same general area.

Stomach. Fatal, but not an advisable or good hit, due to minimal veining and slow blood loss. Way too much chance of losing the animal.

Spine. If arrow severs the spinal column, then it is an outstanding shot because the animal goes down instantly. If no severing, minor wound. Hit in front half of body often will kill animal outright; hit in back half causes loss of control of hindquarters, requires another shot. The sooner the better, because this is one of the less-pleasant aspects of poor-good hits.

Front Quarters. Not anywhere near as good a hit as first appears. Usually dramatic blood loss with the hit, but almost always trails off to nothing. Mostly a superficial hit, poor shot. A heavy draw-weight bow, as noted earlier, will go through the shoulder blade of small and medium-sized big game, unless the broadhead hits the ridge. Generally, though, this is the site of more bounce-outs than anywhere else.

Hind Quarters. Hitting the femoral artery which runs down each hind quarter is as effective as hitting the heart. The artery lies next to the bone, toward the midline of the body; in other words, if you're behind the animal and shoot at the right hind quarter, hope that you hit just to the left of that bone. Remainder of ham has plenty of decent-sized blood vessels that, when hit, sometimes can leak enough blood to prove fatal, but this seldom happens.

Shot which misses bone and femoral artery on inside (toward body's midline) may range forward through intestines, liver, diaphragm and heart/lung area but not leave much of a blood trail.

The first whitetail deer killed with bow and arrow during a regular bow season (early 1930's, Wisconsin, by Roy Case) was killed with a shot of this nature. The arrow protruded several inches out the buck's chest.

Shot which passes on outside of bone basically is a deep but superficial wound unless it enters at such an angle that it can range forward into the body.

Rear-end. For want of a better label, rear-end is used. We really mean the upper segment of the hindquarters, the pelvic area and end of the spine. Long tradition vehemently opposes any intentional shot to this area, but reasonable people with experience and thought regarding this have pointed out that a coffee-can-sized area here contains the major artery feeding the femoral arteries and the bases of the femoral arteries where they branch out into each leg, the pelvic bone itself, and the spinal column.

These same bowhunters carefully point out that this is not a shot for everyone. They suggest being able to hit a playing card every time at 20 yards before attempting a shot of this nature because a small error can produce a gut-shot animal that possibly may be difficult to recover.

Best shot angle is from the rear or side, or anywhere quartering between. Not much of a shot from a forward angle.

We're not coming down on either side of the rear shot issue, but are simply passing along the information, for you to do with as you wish.

Head Shot. Poor shot, but if taken from behind the animal so the broadhead penetrates the skull at the base of the spine, it is instantly fatal. I know a New Jersey hunter who killed a nice North Dakota pronghorn that way with an 80-yard shot.

"I didn't really expect to hit it," he said, "but when I did there sure was a cloud of dust stirred up as the buck tumbled."

A shot of this nature is similar to the Hail Mary pass in the last five seconds of a football game and usually occurs in about the same time frame on a bowhunt.

When To Shoot

This is the most difficult segment of bowhunting in which to give suggestions, because it is an area that no matter how much you prepare for and read about and plan for and think about, nothing beats being there and doing it. Sure there are similarities, yet each shot is different. Timing is everything in many activities, and this is one of them.

Remember that two parties are involved in this act, one knowingly and one unknowingly or at least unalarmed knowing. "Be cool" isn't jive here. It may be impossible, but it isn't jive.

Anticipation isn't the whole answer, either...the type which has you saying "When it gets past that bush I'll shoot." Planning the shot in advance is smart, being ready for it is smart, but expecting the animal to cooperate with your plans is asking too much. So you may be better off tracking the animal's movement with your bow, or waiting and watching until it nears a place for a good shot and then gives you an opportunity to draw unseen.

The best advice anyone can give is: "Take the first good shot offered." There are obvious exceptions, such as when you are able to pick and choose from among bears on a bait, or deer in the swamp just outside of town, or you've hit it just right on a big adventure hunt, but most of the time it is a solid general rule.

Trophy hunters and those who think they are trophy hunters routinely ignore this suggestion, too, but theirs are special cases. The guy who has a wall filled with trophies, fine. The starting hunter who thinks he wants to start at the top will do himself a big favor if he takes the first good shot and gets some experience under his belt.

If I had a nickel for every time a bowhunter has passed up a good shot, telling himself that with the way that animal is approaching it will offer a better shot in just a moment, I would be a wealthy person.

So I'll say it again: *"Take the first good shot offered."*

This is especially important on an out-of-state hunt where you expect your opportunities to be limited. If you're strictly on a trophy hunt, then ignore this advice unless that first shot is at a whopper. If you are in a game-rich area where you have almost a certified chance to pick and choose, then ignore this advice. This might be a big Alaskan valley or two with several bull moose to glass over and pick from, or it might be on a caribou hunt that puts you smack in the middle of the migration. In this latter case, there's a good chance you'll need to pass up the first few shots just to give your nerves an opportunity to settle down.

But on a short hunt, or a general hunt which you might not have the opportunity to duplicate soon, *take the first good shot offered*. It might be—and probably will be—the *only* shot offered.

Whether you're in the back pasture or the Brooks Range, when it nears time to fish or cut bait, what do you look for?

Watch the animal's general behavior. Nervous actions are nervous actions. Some are true nervousness, some are built-in defense mechanisms ingrained over the eons. The old and infamous head-bob of the whitetail deer is one, as it drops its head like it is going to feed then raises right back up and catches you in mid-draw. Pronghorns have the same move at a waterhole, dipping their muzzle just long enough for you to begin to draw before lifting their head for the "got'cha" trick.

Note the muscle tension or lack of it. Bunched muscles will show up well under the skin.

Watch the animal's tail, if it has one worth watching. (Try to watch a bear's tail too much and you'll go blind from squinting.) A whitetail deer, for instance, has a wide vocabulary of tail signals, including the slowly rising tail for possible alarm, the straight out tail for thinking about alarm (or an eager doe waiting for a buck, or a buck bird-dogging on an eager doe's scent), the lifted tail for alarm and the wig-wagged tail for all is well. A droopy, do-nothing tail indicates supreme relaxation.

Watch the ears, no matter whether the animal is approaching you or you are stalking in on the animal. Those ears are like independent radar screens, turning here and there to pick up and analyze sounds. Ears at half mast, for want of a better term, show a relaxed animal. Ears swiveling together are zeroing in on something. And, of course, when the ears and the eyes concentrate on the same thing, the jig may be up. At the very least, some serious analyzing is taking place.

When the animal is within range, then you'll naturally look for the moment when its head is turned, or it is looking ahead of you. You may need to wait for the near foreleg to move forward to open up the chest for a shot, so watch that leg if needed and try to anticipate its movement. When it moves you won't have much time to shoot.

No matter what the animal, if it takes time to scratch or lick itself, it is relaxed.

Be sure to estimate the speed of the animal's approach. A feeding animal wanders in and out of range, but at least it is relaxed. A walking animal may not be alarmed or concerned about anything, but it won't give you as much time to get ready and act. The first time I saw a walking elk, I couldn't believe the ground it covered in such little time.

Remember that a moving animal is less able to pick out movement than is a standing animal, simply because the moving animal's entire surroundings are in motion. Your motion, unless it is radically different or blatantly obvious, has a better chance of passing unnoticed.

This is why it is such a good trick to move when an animal is startled into sudden flight, especially if that animal is of the circling kind, such as a whitetail deer. If you're on the ground and spook the animal, dash downwind as it dashes away. It will stop as soon as it feels safe further back in the cover, and then it probably will begin circling downwind to figure out what startled it. If you have moved downwind, chances are it may circle in front of you and have its attention directed away from you and further upwind. This is *not* a weird suggestion. Many hunters have made it work for them.

With pronghorns, once they dip their muzzle into the water and begin drinking hard enough that you can see their throat ripple and their sides bellow in and out, they are concentrating on one thing only—getting enough water. You had better shoot then, because when they quit drinking they often quit in a hurry and leave in a hurry, as if they suddenly remembered they were late for an appointment.

Black bears have a false rush, wherein they suddenly look up from the bait, look around, then dash 10 to 12 yards, stop instantly and look around to see if they have provoked anything into charging them or into flight. If nothing happens, they figure things are all right and return to the bait. Then they tend to relax quite a bit.

Although you should strongly consider taking the first good shot you get under most circumstances, *don't force the shot*. This is not a contradiction. The animal may have seen or heard or smelled something it wants to check out, so it looks in your direction. Or it may be making a routine surveillance and just happens to look in your direction. Either way, you're probably convinced the animal has you cold.

The urge is to draw and shoot. That is the wrong urge most of the time. You know you're there, but the animal may not. Wait it out and let the animal's next movement or movements tell you what to do. With the animal looking in your direction, your odds are poor anyway. The best you can hope for, really, is a quick shot at a fleeing animal. Once in a while you may need to draw s-l-o-w-l-y when indications are that it is now or never, but that's why it's called hunting instead of a sure thing.

Don't Be Afraid To Shoot

The statements relative to shooting or not shooting are interesting. Some would-be bowhunters are afraid to miss. That is understandable, because they equate missing with failure. But you can't learn unless you try, and failure comes with trying. And you can't put brown on the ground unless you get an arrow into the air. This is not advocating willy-nilly arrow flinging. What it is advocating is forgetting about missing—everyone misses—and forgetting about the cost of arrows. You obviously want only high-percentage shots, but you can't tag it if you don't shoot at it.

Did you pick your spots? How did your choices compare? Even expert bowhunters would disagree on the "best" shot in each situation.

Buck is well posed for a shot at the lungs . . . If you are at full draw when it begins looking at you, and IF the animal is not nervous. This one certainly is paying attention. It doesn't show much bodily tension, and its ears are in their normal position. Sometimes you can come to full draw on a pronghorn and get off a good shot, even if it watches you draw, if you make the move slowly enough. If the animal is not alarmed, you can get a good shot on it in this position if the range isn't too long. The alarm factor is the important variable here, because a pronghorn can move from an arrow's path with lightning-like speed. A much better shot would be at an animal which has its head down, as when drinking or feeding. Remember, too, that a pronghorn is a smallish big game animal, which means that there's a good chance you can shoot through the shoulder blade and still get good penetration.

This appears to be an excellent shot opportunity if you can get your arrow between the two branches. Think of those branches as a frame highlighting the lung area instead of barriers to your shot. This should help your mental control. The arrow path quarters nicely into the lungs. Since the animal is quartering away, remember to adjust your point of impact back a bit on the elk's side so the arrow will range forward into the lungs. A good way to figure the best point of entry is to visually draw an imaginary line from you to the animal's far foreleg. This should see the arrow ranging forward through the lungs.

A frontal shot is always a tough shot, physically and conditionally. The animal often has a clear view of you and may already have seen you draw. It may be tense, ready to flee at any alarm. That's the conditional part. This angle gives the animal the most protection from shoulder blades, heavy rib bones and big muscle. Tense muscle is always more dense than relaxed muscle and thus more difficult to penetrate. Best effort for this angle is to aim just to the left of the base of the throat at the neck and body juncture for the heart. If that isn't practical aim higher on the body so the arrow can go inside the shoulder blade and range through the ribs down into the lungs, possibly also cutting diaphragm and ranging back into the liver. If you have an exit hole on the bottom of the deer, you should have an easy trail. If there is no exit hole, it may be an extremely difficult trail.

The moose is a thick-skinned, heavy boned animal. This is an excellent quartering-away angle, for you want your arrow to enter behind the rib cage and range forward through the diaphragm and into the lungs. On a low shot, the arrow might also catch liver before it punctures the diaphragm and might catch the heart as well as lungs. Try to get your arrow to fly just past the right hind leg and then into the boiler room.

This buck is half a step from offering you a perfect walking shot. As soon as it moves its right foreleg forward, exposing its lungs/heart region, the shot will be perfect. But you have to anticipate that forward motion and allow for it or you might end up with a gut shot.

Remember that the heart/lung cavity on an animal cannot be completely full of lungs at all times, because the lungs need space to expand as the animal inhales. Thus, if you shoot an arrow high through the lung cavity when the lungs are smallest—while the animal exhales—you will administer nothing more than a flesh wound on each side of the animal. The shot will look great; it will zip right through the animal. But you will have hit what is called "no man's land" and will have learned definitely to aim low, aim low, aim low.

Tempting, but. . . . Frontal angle is not good, especially since this an extremely heavily muscled animal. Second ram is partially behind the lead ram's body, so an arrow glancing off bone could also wound the second animal, which is not what you want. This situation almost says "Wait for a better shot." But if you are at full draw, all you need do is release the arrow, and if the animals are as relaxed as they appear, you could well get your arrow into the lead ram's heart/lung region by shooting slightly above the base of the neck, above the brisket a few inches. Remember that the heart doesn't lay tight to the bottom of the cavity but is instead somewhat surrounded by lung lobe, which helps it ride higher. A shot here could catch the heart, some of the lungs but not much, puncture the diaphragm and maybe the liver. If there is an exit hole, trailing might be easy; if not, trailing may be quite difficult.

Frontal shots are difficult at all times, but especially so on an enraged, tensed bull elk bugling a warning to you. Neck muscles are not enlarged and engorged, muscles are tense, the bone structure is heavy. A possible shot location is noted, but this seems to be a time when it is best to wait and see what develops. The bull might turn and offer an excellent shot as it turns. If it turns too swiftly to offer a good shot, you might be able to call it back again or follow it and try another setup. Of course, we don't know from this photo whether the bull has spotted you. If you are well hidden, this could move conditions a bit in your favor since the bull may move only a little bit after concluding its bugle.

Note the ears. The buck's attention is directed at something other than you. That's in your favor. It does not appear to be unduly alarmed, just checking out something, so that's in your favor.

Best shot here is just to the left or ahead of the left front shoulder. Your arrow should range through the lungs and, if low enough, should penetrate the heart. The left lung lobe is well protected by the left shoulder, but if you run your arrow through the flesh of the forward part of the left front shoulder you may well catch the left lung lobe as well as the heart and right lung lobe. Secondary shot here would be to go in extremely tight behind the left front shoulder, catching the left lung lobe, puncturing the diaphragm and the liver. Trouble with this one is that if you're off left, you hit the shoulder blade, and if you're off right, you get a gut shot. The gut shot is never wanted. The shoulder blade shot may not be troublesome if your bow/arrow setup has enough kinetic energy to penetrate the shoulder blade and the vitals behind it. Going through the blade part won't be as troublesome as the main vertical ridge of the bone which is much thicker.

A bedded animal is relaxed, which is in your favor. You might be able to get an arrow into the vitals by aiming for an impact point just above and to the right of the visual V formed by the juncture of the right hip bone and the short ribs, or just behind the short ribs right next to the spinal column and just over the hip. Your arrow could range into the vitals without hitting any bone and could well emerge out the chest for a good blood trail. However, much of the ram's vitals are protected by spinal column bone and hip bone. Shoot too high and your arrow will go above the lungs. As it is, the appearance given is one of the probably catching only the right lung lobe, and too high at that. Trying to sever the spine is always a chancy shot.

If at all possible, the hunter should move higher and left or right, preferably right if the terrain permits, for a better angle at the vitals.

A shot could be taken from this angle but may not be the best shot available. The animal is treed. You can move around for a much better shot angle, one which would not have a snow-laden branch obscuring part of the animal's vitals and its shoulder covering additional vital area. On the other hand, if this is the best shot offered, aim at the spot and do it. Your arrow will clear the snow on the branch and will strike mid-lung just behind the shoulder blade.

10

Scouting Your Way To Bow Hunting Success

Since you're a member of the North American Hunting Club, you're already a hunter. You know the value of tracks, trails, rubbed trees, scrapes, evidence of feeding, individual animal sightings, wallows, droppings and other signs of animal presence. You automatically check for the freshness of sign.

Now, as a bowhunter, you must become more yardage-specific in your scouting and hunting-setup efforts. You must become a better amateur biologist to learn additional traits of the game. You must become a bit of a farmer/rancher to pick up details on food sources. You must become a better weatherman.

You try to pinpoint specific movement patterns better. You pay closer attention to the effects of weather, cover, existence and location of food sources, widths of cover that animals move through. "About there" is not good enough any more. "Right here" is the new rule.

Seasons Within A Season

You become more aware of seasons within seasons. A two or three month bowhunting season for whitetails is a perfect example.

The deer should still be in their summer movement patterns on opening weekend, unless the area has been so thoroughly disrupted by bowhunters trying to cram all their scouting into two weeks just prior to the season.

After this, deer retreat to heavier cover and increased nocturnal movement. Then the young bucks start moving around, as they sense the increase in reproductive hormones. Maybe older, wiser bucks begin moving more too, but they certainly aren't as visible as the youngsters. You'll see these youngsters chasing around on the main trails with does and fawns.

When the does come into heat, activity intensifies for all bucks and does. Before the peak, there's a lot of running around while does tell bucks "not yet."

During the peak of rut, deer seem to be all over the place all the time, day and night. Cold snaps and heat spells will modify this.

When the rut slows down, bucks tend to disappear. Some disappear during the bow season, too, and some during the gun season. Others just fade back into cover.

Then comes the late season and the smaller rut a month after the main rut.

There also is strong possibility that minor ruts are appropriately spaced for a couple of months *before* the peak of the rut, each with their corresponding increase in activity.

For good measure, toss in food changes. When the acorns drop, forget most everything else. When the persimmons drop, forget anything else. Every area has its own example.

With a wet season, vegetation is lush. Cover is better. Deer don't need to move far for food. It's a new ballgame.

Add the opening of squirrel season, or grouse season, or pheasant season. The people hunting those species disrupt deer movement patterns.

Add a killing frost which removes a lot of food. Later on the harvesting of crops and their removal from the food source.

How do you cope? You scout with brain working and eyes open, then you scout some more. Then some more.

This is the homework. The test comes when you tell yourself, "Today, I'm hunting."

This is only one example for only one species, but you get the idea.

You can know all you need to know about your bow and shooting it accurately on the target and field ranges. You can read all there is to read about bowhunting. You can listen to bowhunters talk about the things they do which help make them *consistently* successful. But your own bowhunting education doesn't really begin until you head into the field to scout out the intended quarry for the following season—and for several seasons afterward.

Before you do that, you have decisions to make and homework to do.

What are your goals? Trophy-class animal, any antlered/horned animal, any legal animal? This decision gets you on the right road. It also helps you plan and later scout *with a purpose*. You cannot plan right, scout right or hunt right if you have no purpose other than a general one. Also, when a shot presents itself, you may not have time to debate whether or not to take it unless you have already established your guidelines.

Now, when you check with Department of Natural Resources biologists and other personnel for game habitats, populations, sex ratios, trophy areas, ease or difficulty of getting into certain areas, etc., you can ask the right questions.

Also ask of other open seasons. Two years ago on a Colorado elk hunt, neither my partner nor I thought to ask that question until we got there and noticed that muzzleloader elk season was open at the same time as bow season in our area. This did not help our hunt. Gave us good practice, however, bugling other hunters to us.

The Pope & Young Club record book will pinpoint trophy areas, too. Note the year taken. Areas are not static. Some improve while others weaken. Update what you find.

When you check with farmers, ranchers, biologists, other bowhunters, cattle truck drivers, rural mail carriers, school bus drivers, or anyone who may be familiar with the area you would like to hunt or who travels a lot in that area, you can get the best information.

Get topographical maps of the areas you plan to hunt. If you're looking at private land, get plat books to find out who owns what.

If possible, fly over the area. This is a common occurrence in Alaska and parts of Canada and the western United States, but it can work just as well when scouting for whitetails in brush country. Winter flying, especially in snow country, will quickly show cover areas, trails, feeding areas. Take photos and compare the photos to your maps.

Year-round Scouting

If you can, scout year round. Winter scouting will confirm things you saw from the air. Spring scouting, especially in snow country where animals remain in their main territory year round, can be highly informative. With grass and leaves flattened by snow, and vegetation not yet budded, you can see every nuance in changes of elevation, every little dip or depression that can hide an

In snow country, spring scouting can reveal game trails and other aspects of the terrain that would be less noticeable once the soil dries and foliage appears.

animal's movement. Best time to do your spring scouting is immediately after the snow melts. The ground will show sign—created last fall and preserved by the snow—prominently while it is moist. When the soil dries, forget it. The highlights disappear.

Spring is an excellent time to trim branches, saplings or brush from the trees you select as good treestand sites and from shooting lanes between the trees and trails. Scars on the trees will be dull and not noticeable by fall, and any disruption you caused the game will be long forgotten.

Collecting shed antlers is an enjoyable pastime *and* a good way to scout for deer during the late winter and early spring.

Summer scouting tells you where the animals are and most likely will be when the season opens. In agricultural areas, you will know which crops are in the same locations and which are now in different fields. You can watch the growing trophies and learn to identify them.

This is an excellent time to learn how animals move, how their muscles show when tense or relaxed, how much or little time you may have when drawing on them during the season to make a shot. If you cannot do this, go to a zoo and observe the appropriate species there. A few years ago my kids and I were watching a bull elk when one of the kids tried a high-pitched keening tone. That bull tipped his muzzle in the air and let loose a bugle that startled everyone. We were informed by a uniformed person who hastened up that the act was not to be repeated. Probably broke some city noise code.

Any time animals can be patterned they should be patterned. That is your key to later ambush, whether on foot or from a treestand. Big whitetails, for instance, are difficult to pattern, but the best time to try is late summer while they still are in summer movement patterns and during the late season (usually December) in snow country.

Gun season can be the best time to discover an animal's primary escape routes and bedding areas. That's the time of greatest human pressure, and you can bet the animals will be looking for the best cover as fast as possible.

Scouting will continue right during hunting season. We obviously learn as we hunt, filing that information for later reference, maybe for this season, maybe for next season or seasons after that.

For instance, you saw a good buck pull a successful escape maneuver out of a certain spot next to a cornfield three years ago. That field didn't have corn the next two years, so conditions changed. This year it has corn again. If the deer is still there, it will still be fully aware of its past successful maneuver. But so are you, and you can plan to shortstop it this time. Different deer may like this same escape route.

The last thing we want to do, however, is try to do both scouting and hunting at the same time and do justice to both. It cannot be done. Scout when you scout and hunt when you hunt.

If you have several preferred areas, each of which is good under certain wind directions or food availability, scout these areas on a well-spaced but regular basis during the season until the right time or conditions arrive to hunt them. Then *hunt* them.

Late bow season can be tough because of cold weather, but often the rewards are worth the difficulties. Late seasons in the

Scouting just before and during the hunting season pays obvious dividends, you know where the animals are at the time. But be prepared to change your tactics if other factors influence their patterns.

mountains usually see animals bunched together, and the animals are more visible. These same conditions mean scouting for next week and next year can be excellent, too.

Notebook

There is no way all the information you run through your brain can be remembered. Too many details. Too many little incidents, short items, tips, asides, variations.

So do yourself and your hunting results a favor. Keep a notebook.

Over the years, it will build into an exciting diary, to be read and reread for information and for pleasure. Your notebook will show you patterns and behavioral responses of the animals which you will have forgotten. It will show you the time of month various things happen, which will help you time your hunting efforts properly.

What You Need To Know

Certain things are basic to all scouting efforts:

1) Know as much as possible about the animal you plan to hunt, its size and habits and foods.

2) Know as much as possible about the home ground of the animal you will be hunting—valleys, saddles, draws, dips, depressions, swamps, crop fields, mountains, ditchbanks, benches, thickets, grass fields, fencerows, dry streambeds, mast crop food sources, and on and on.

In fact, the second point is so important that if you know it well you can fairly reasonably predict where animals might travel and when they might travel there...then get yourself set up in advance instead of being forced into playing continual catch-up.

Knowing the terrain thoroughly is of benefit, especially in hunting the secretive, reclusive whitetail deer. You know *tendencies* and *influences*. You know (because you have seen them) or suspect that good-size animals move through a certain area or areas. However, hunting one specific animal is almost impossible, and it can be self-defeating if you zero in on too few spots. You may spook the animal without a glimpse of it.

Almost always you will have better results if you hunt a given general area, hunt good bucks in that area, if you are trophy hunting. Your chances are better for having one of them pass your stand within range.

We seldom are aware of all the good bucks in an area. Talk

Scouting/hunting in big country like the West requires different techniques than you would use in other regions of North America. Usually you must locate the animals first, before you can hunt them.

with any bowhunter who is consistently successful on trophy deer and if he is honest he will tell you he took many of those bucks the first or second time he saw them. Their territories overlap, and they move more than we are inclined to think they do.

This factor is particularly true when the habitat is not concentrated. When deer have more movement options, you need to give yourself more options.

Actually, no matter what species you are hunting, going after one specific animal tends to make us so singular in our thoughts and actions that we can mess up what otherwise would be excellent opportunities at good animals. When we limit our options we set ourselves up for failure.

The major difference between Eastern/Midwestern/Southern hunting and hunting in bigger country is that in the big country you must find the animals before you can hunt them, whereas in the other areas you can be hunting the instant you step out your door.

Eastern/Midwestern/Southern/ bowhunters have whitetail deer, black bear and turkey as resident species, with the black bear not nearly as widespread as the other two species. Further west and further north, the number of huntable species increases tremendously.

If you live in one area and intend someday to hunt the other type of area, remember this huge difference and you will do much better in your scouting and your hunting. I felt overwhelmed the first time I hunted the West, and a western friend of mine got a severe case of claustrophobia when I talked him into hunting heavy timber in brush so thick you couldn't see 15 yards. Even though he had muleys everywhere, he had to get back to the country where he could see into next month.

The mark of a good hunter is to be able to know an animal and its traits well enough that he can study the topo maps for a *new area*, ask a few questions and come up with a quick, very well educated guess regarding the better places to hunt.

That is the difference between having 20 years of hunting experience and 20 repetitions of the same experience.

Bob Fratzke, Winona, Minnesota, is one of the better whitetail deer scouts I know. He says, ''You're trying to learn all you can about some animal's, or group of animals', house and frontyard. That takes work and thought. Gradually, if you do it right, you'll start seeing repetitions of certain things. Patterns will come together, and you'll start predicting pretty closely what might happen. It's still hunting, a long way from a sure thing, but it makes you feel pretty good when you go with a hunch and the hunch pays off. It's satisfying taking the animal, but just as satisfying knowing that you had the knowledge to put all the signs together and go to the right place at the right time. If you do that often enough, people will begin to think you're one of the luckiest hunters around.''

Attitude

The right attitude is important. You must have confidence in your ability to prove or disprove to yourself that the area you want to scout will be a good place to hunt. Secondly, you must have confidence that if the area looks to be worthy of spending more time there, you can find places to put yourself in high-percentage shot situations in bow range.

This is nothing more than positive thinking, but that is quite a bit.

This confidence/no confidence factor can be more of a problem for a bowhunter looking for game in heavy cover, simply because the game cannot be seen as easily, often or well. As a human animal with poor noses, decent ears and very good eyesight, we are primarily visually oriented. The cliche reads "Seeing is believing."

Anyone who hunts in heavy cover is much more dependent upon sign—evidence of feeding, trails, tracks, droppings, etc.— than the bowhunter who can set up just below the crest of a ridge and spend a couple of hours with binoculars and spotting scope looking for game to go after. The big country hunter sighs and says, "Well, if they aren't in this valley, they might be in the next one. Better go look." The thick-cover hunter sighs and says, "Geez, they gotta be here somewhere. Or don't they? I wonder where they've moved. Maybe they haven't. Maybe too many people have been through here."

Maybe...maybe...maybe.

The comparison with fishing—wherein 10 percent of the water holds the fish and the other 90 percent helps fill the lake—is inescapable. The comparison is more dramatic in big country hunting, I believe. In eastern brush country, where you're speaking mostly of whitetail deer, you think right if you compare them to cottontail rabbits. Both can and do hide in the dangedest little pockets of cover, places where no sensible, self-respecting animal would be.

Corollary to this is that not every piece of vegetation is food for the animals. Some is as barren, for game, as a pile of sand.

So...when you are working in the tight confines of brush country, where the viewing generally is short and the game can be upon you before you know it (or vice versa), where the anticipation factor can be a huge plus or a huge minus, confidence in yourself and your scouting abilities is a must.

"The danged things haven't left the country. So I just have to figure out where they are, what they're doing and when."

Yup, that's all. Piece of cake—until you get frustrated. I talked to a fellow at a bowhunting show a couple of years ago who told me, "I saw more game and got more shots when I knew a lot less about bowhunting."

Why? He isn't the only one to encounter this problem. Based on conversations with hundreds of bowhunters at dozens of shows, I'd say the problem is created by having too many ideas in theory and not enough in practice. You can cram your mind so full of

Whitetails have been feeding in this cornfield, but knowing just that is not enough. You need to evaluate other things such as what time of day or night do they feed; which direction do they travel from; and is the area still being actively used. Knowledge and confidence in your scouting abilities are a vital part to a successful hunt.

great things gleaned from seminars and conversations and magazines and videos that they're impossible to sort out. You know of so many options you mentally paralyze yourself.

The only solution is to go back to basics: Animals need to eat, remain safe and as comfortable as possible, and reproduce their species. They need to move around to accomplish these things. Various factors affect how and what they do, and when they do it.

That's all there is...plus paying attention to the wind at all times.

Fred Bear mentioned something to me years ago that should be instantly obvious but isn't. "Roughly 50 weeks of the year, the animal's entire existence is governed by his belly. He wants to keep it full. Those other two weeks, the breeding season, are an important part of hunting season for some species, but some species are not bowhunted during their rut. Which means that all our efforts to find a shootable member of these latter species is entirely concentrated in figuring out what to do when he is smartest—when all he is thinking about is his belly."

The more you know of the species' preferred foods, ability to identify them, where they are and when the game feeds on them, the better your scouting and hunting results will be.

When you're scouting, what you see is not always what you get. This is because your eyes may see things that your brain does not, when you really should be seeing like a camera—every detail. This isn't easy to do; it takes training.

Since we have great memories, we tend to remember all sorts of things good and bad. That's fine *if* we also remember to keep an open mind and a flexible attitude. Unfortunately, too often we use the words "always" and "never" when trying to figure out or predict game behavior. That is wrong, a symptom of tunnel vision and a closed mind.

Since conditions change, we must *see what is in front of us right now*, not just what we want to see or not see.

Wild animals are habitual creatures, true. However, they also react instantly to changes and pressures. For instance, when a farmer rotates his crop fields, the deer rotate to the new locations for corn, alfalfa, soybeans, etc. When foliage drops, movement patterns will change. When snow gets too deep for animals to dig for food, they move. When the water holes dry up, they move. When an apartment building is built in a bedding area, they move. When the wind is too strong for comfort, they get out of the wind to an acceptable comfort level. When bird hunters or small game hunters or other human intrusion bothers them, they move. When the weather is hot, they find the coolest places. When insects bother them, they find a breezy place.

Not all movements are geographical. Some are time oriented— the animals simply become more nocturnal. This reaction is almost exclusively in response to human pressure.

We need to be aware of those movements *and* their causes. We need to be aware of the potential for movement before it actually happens, so we can adjust at the right time instead of an instant too late.

Consider the ripple effect in scouting. Any and all areas we hunt have influences (such as those mentioned three paragraphs ago) within the areas *and* beyond the areas. Animal territories move and change with breeding season, food sources, water availability, habitat disappearance, etc. They and other factors just outside the area(s) we intend to hunt affect animal presence and living patterns in our hunting area.

So we need to scout as far as practical beyond the area we plan to hunt. We may not hunt the edge of a cornfield two miles away or whatever the distance, but if animals moving through our hunting area use that field as a primary food source, we had better know of its existence and when it is harvested. If there's an oak ridge with a heavy acorn crop off the land we can hunt, and the oaks are of a species the game animals like, we won't see much back in the heavy brush when the acorns drop.

A big part of the reason we need to be aware of the ripple effect is that we usually think too small, zeroing in on a specific area or field or tree or meadow or trail or neck of timber or mountain pass. When we cultivate this tunnel vision we tend to over-use those particular areas we prefer. We get lazy.

We are way ahead of the pack if we train ourselves to think big, even in heavy cover. We know that in heavy cover, alarmed animals will often circle and remain in the area, (except for some mountain country animals, such as elk, which start running and keep on running until they are a couple of valleys and ridges away), but that is not the condition we need to be most concerned about here.

Our major concern should be that *we are the most patterned and patternable animal afield*. We are as habitual as wild animals—more so. When we zero in on too few hunting places we disturb them too much with our presence. We present too many

Getting an aerial view of your hunting spot and the country around it is an excellent way to evaluate the ripple effect in your scouting and hunting efforts.

opportunities for game to see us. We leave too much of our scent behind.

When this is the problem, we quite possibly have a fine case of tunnel vision. We have lost our flexibility, our adaptability. We have probably shot ourselves out of the saddle.

The question is often asked by bowhunters in areas where the game seemingly can be hunted anywhere: How many times should I consecutively sit at a stand before giving up on it, or giving up on it in that time frame?

Rule of thumb used to be three times, such as three consecutive evenings or consecutive mornings.

That has been improved upon. Today, you will find that most of the consistently successful bowhunters—especially those who consistently take trophy-class animals—rarely sit in a particular stand two consecutive times in the woods.

This is simply because they do not want to over-use an area, stink it up, warn the animals. They will have many good locations scouted and ready. The law of averages works in reverse when you pollute an area.

Yes, there are stands which are consistently successful year after year, but I'm willing to bet that those stands are not equally good at any time of the bowhunting season, especially if the season is more than a couple of weeks long and/or includes climatic changes.

Yes, bear hunters go back to the same bait and same stand day after day, with success. Bears know the hunter is there 99 times out of 100 and usually couldn't care less. Big bears are accustomed to being the boss, and subordinate bears are accustomed to worry only about more-dominant bears.

Yes, there are exceptions to every rule. Also, blindly following rules of thumb too closely often results in broken thumbs, figuratively speaking. See what you need to see. Be mentally flexible at all times. If the game is there, it is there; if it isn't, it isn't, despite the fond memories you may have of that place or the sign you saw there the last time you checked.

Here's an excellent example of the "don't over-use a spot" principle. Whitetail deer hunters often note that the most deer or largest-antlered deer (or both) are seen at a particular location the first time that location is hunted. This happens often enough that it is not coincidental.

The reason for this is simple, the deer have no prior alarms at this particular location. No bad human smell, no threatening

Whitetails are going through this open corridor in the brush, but for how long? Could human intrusion in the area eventually re-route their movements?

gestures or missed shots or woundings. Nothing. The area seems safe to them. They travel through, and they are relaxed. If you have set up properly, with maybe a bit of luck riding along, you just might pop that big buster. If not, well, that's why it's called hunting.

Human disturbance can create corridors of game movement through that game's territory. In fact, our movement *does* create corridors.

Before we intrude, such as to do some heavy scouting just before hunting season, the animals were reasonably relaxed, or as relaxed as they are ever going to be. When we enter the scene, we or our scent collide with game at various points. If the animals cannot accept that, they will stay away from those particular locations the next time they move through, or they move through there at night, or they check it out thoroughly before attempting to move through at any time.

In effect, we re-route the animals.

However, if the animal moves safely through an area, it will go through that area again and again until it dies of old age, it is spooked out of the area—or you set up unknown to it and put an arrow where you want it.

11

Modern
Bowhunting Techniques

Hunting techniques for bowhunting are no different from any
other hunting techniques. There is a difference, however,
between a person carrying bowhunting equipment and a bowhunter. Sometimes the progression from the former to the latter is
slow, painful, frustrating, agonizing, humbling or humiliating.
Sometimes, it's all of the above.

On the other hand, when you pull it off and tag an animal,
there's no greater sense of satisfaction and pride of accomplish-
ment. You took on a special challenge, the challenge of the bow,
and you did it right.

This is why you will hear bowhunters say that *any* game taken
with a bow can and should be considered a trophy.

In bowhunting, you can stillhunt, stalk, drive game, stand or
use dogs (for some species).

Bowhunting Techniques
Stillhunting. Stillhunting as defined here, means slow, careful
movement through terrain in search of animals to stalk. It isn't
easy. You have more ways of messing up than when you're on a
stand, much of which is caused by the simple fact we have trouble
gearing down to the snail's pace needed. You must watch the
wind, foot placement, other wildlife which might give alarm,
vegetative cover which can brush against you with a scrape, insects

which might harass, etc. This is a prime situation for the use of bowhunter math. That's where 99 things done right minus one thing done wrong equals zero, not 98.

The most difficult part of stillhunting and stalking is gearing yourself down to the slow, careful movement. This is the epitome of paying attention to details. You can make noises, because there are natural sounds in the woods, but those noises you make had better sound like something harmless.

The animal really has the advantage in stillhunting, because you have no idea where it might be. This places a premium on slow, careful movement.

Stillhunting and stalking place a premium on the right type of sole material on your footwear. The soles must be soft. They must not have deep lugs. Hard, deep-lugged soles are inflexible and insensitive, and they catch on rocks and twigs and other items which we cannot feel. A good sole material must allow you to feel the ground a good bit, because you cannot always be looking at the ground to see where to place each foot.

Footwear also must blend with the cover, so if you want to wear tennies for their softness and sensitivity, be sure they are a dark, dull color and don't have twinkly eyelets.

Some of the best stillhunters and stalkers I know carry a couple pairs of heavy, dark wool socks with them at all times. When they begin stillhunting or stalking, they either pull a pair of socks over their footwear or remove the boots and pull on the socks. If they anticipate rougher, uncomfortable foot placement, they will pull both pairs on. This gives the best in silence and in protection of our tender feet.

Stillhunting works well on relatively unpredictable animals in heavy cover, such as moose, blacktail deer, mule deer, wild hogs and javelina. It also works on the relatively-predictable whitetail if luck is with you. There are ways of being consistently successful stillhunting with a gun for whitetails, but when you pick up the bow your chances of success are almost laughable.

The term 'predictable' applies in hunting as this: *A predictable animal is a dead animal, and just when you think a particular animal is predictable it does something unpredictable.*

Stillhunting is most successful when animals are feeding or moving easily for other reasons. Early mornings and late afternoons, then, are the best times. Don't discount mid-day, however, because even though most animals are bedded then—and a bedded animal is awfully tough to get close to—many animals will get up, move around some, feed awhile and lie back down. Sort of like a light exercise and snack time.

One of the most effective ways of stillhunting whitetails is in cornfields. Hunt cross-row, into the wind or quartering it. Stick your head into the row ahead of you, look both ways. If you see a bedded or feeding deer, back up three or four rows and move down the row until you approach within shot range. If you see no deer, move ahead one row and look again. You can criss-cross the field in this manner, hunting into the wind.

Deer tend to relax in this dense cover, and they can be comfortably cool in there, with few insects. The rustling of cornstalk leaves in a breeze is quite constant, so that rustling does not make them nervous like the rustling of brush and tree leaves. That's good, because the only time to hunt a cornfield this way is during breezy or windy conditions.

If you hunt a cornfield, obviously get permission first, and then be careful to retrieve any arrow shot. You do not want that arrow to end up in a tractor tire or corn chopper.

Stillhunting can be exhausting, for it requires intense concentration at all times. When you are, in essence, stalking blindly, you cannot ever let down. But you can develop the necessary control to concentrate without being wired. If you're wired, you can involuntarily move at the instant game is sighted. If you're concentrating but muscularly relaxed, you will be much better off.

Interesting things happen as you move onto game or game moves onto you, and either can happen. I once spotted two whitetail does feeding in pines and squatted because I knew I couldn't hold still long in the unbalanced pose I was in when I saw them. One doe saw my squatting movement but nothing more. She snorted at me 49 times—I counted—and then moved slowly out of sight. The deer I wanted showed only its rump as it sneaked directly away from me about the time the doe made her third snort.

Every Eastern, Midwestern and Southern bowhunter I know would love to be a better stillhunter and stalker, but their home hunting conditions are not favorable. Stillhunting will drive you crazy as well as into exhaustion when you aren't sure where you will find the animal, and whether you will see it for one second before it makes two steps and is out of sight again.

I've found the best way for me to stillhunt silently is to climb into a canoe and float a little stream. This can produce excellent action at game crossing the stream or bedded nearby. Chunks of

During breezy weather conditions, stillhunting in a cornfield for whitetails can be very profitable.

land inside a U-shaped bend can be driven, with the driver getting out upstream and the stander taking the canoe around the bend and waiting at an appropriate place.

A canoe also is an excellent means of slipping into the backside of good country for standing. It is the farthest from roads in the area, and the game could well be concentrated back there where they have moved to avoid hunting pressure coming in from the road.

Stalking. Stalking is the art—if it isn't considered an art, it ought to be—of sneaking in on a specific animal or animals which has/have been spotted.

Stalking has to be the most gut-wrenching style of bowhunting. Any time you spot game at long range and then attempt to get close enough to it to put an arrow through its boiler room, you've set yourself a challenge. A time consuming, nerve prickling, cautious, careful challenge. It's different from waiting patiently and suddenly having the animal appear from nowhere to be instantly within bow range. Both are exciting, but different.

Stalking is best in reasonably open country where you can get up high and use binoculars and spotting scope. When an animal is spotted, you watch and try to predict its movement over the time expected to reach it. This can involve a lot of distance, circling around and sneaking up draws and such. The movement all has to be careful, because you don't want to stumble onto unseen animals which can spook and ruin your intended setup.

Stalking works best in morning and evening when animals are moving a little bit but not a lot. Fast-moving animals can remove themselves from your intended stalk before it really begins. That usually happens toward the end of feeding time when the animals decide to bed down or head for water.

Another factor about the time animals quit feeding in the morning is the thermal change. I watched a friend sneak on a couple of nice mule deer on a Utah slope one time. He was careful at the start and things looked fine. I could see him angling to the side and increasing his pace, though, as time passed. The animals suddenly looked at him, then melted into the trees.

When he returned, he explained, "I looked at my watch and knew I had only about half an hour before the wind would switch upward and blow my scent right to them. So I tried to get around them and up to that pass in the quakies just up behind them, hoping to time the wind switch and their movement right.

He sat down, drank a slug of water and grinned.

Treestands are the most popular form of stand hunting used by bowhunters today. Notice that this stand is in a tree clump, which helps to hide the hunter from several directions.

"It almost worked."

Standing. Standing is self-explanatory. It includes treestands (natural and man-made, permanent and portable) and ground blinds. Ground blinds can be at ground level or hole blinds. Standing takes place along trails, in general movement areas, at waterholes and wallows, in feeding areas. It may or may not include baits positioned within good shooting range. This style of bowhunting is most often practiced where animal movement patterns are relatively predictable and frequent.

Treestands will be discussed in detail elsewhere, for they are used so predominantly today. In fact, many of today's younger bowhunters quite possibly have seldom, if ever, hunted from a ground blind and most certainly not from a hole blind. That is their misfortune, for each has much to offer.

Ground blinds can be set up quickly. You can drape a length of camo netting around two or three saplings, with a bush or tree at your back, and have an effective position. You can cut saplings, branches and weeds and stick them in the ground in a semi-circle in front of you. (Use a hand pruning shears, available at any hardware

Camo netting draped around saplings makes a good ground blind. A ground blind must be large enough to allow silent movement of bow and drawing arm, and the ground should be cleared of leaves and twigs to eliminate making any noise. You must be hidden from all sides.

store or garden supply house, to make an angled cut. The items will push into the soil much easier.)

Ground blinds can be as elaborate as you wish to make them. However plain or fancy, they must all have one factor—room enough fore and aft to draw your bow without rustling against vegetation.

Ground blinds can consist simply of sitting in front of a bush, rock, tree or whatever offers cover. It is more important to have a solid background than plenty of foreground cover. This applies whether you are in a pitblind at a pronghorn waterhole in Wyoming or an oak brush blind in New York waiting to ambush a huge whitetail.

The ideal is to have good cover behind and in front, but if you cannot have the ideal, analyze each situation and decide. Obviously, with no foreground cover you have to be especially

You're at eye and scent level with the game in a hole blind, but you are also protected from weather and well camouflaged. Any movement at this height is more natural to game and usually is less alarming. Hole blinds need to be prepared in advance, so the smell of freshly-turned soil is gone.

careful of the timing and amount of your movement when you want to shoot at an animal, but that applies anytime. You will just be more conscious of it at ground level.

Clear the ground of anything which can make noise when you move your feet, and have a comfortable seat.

A ground blind with a dugout for your feet is known as a "Hole blind." This allows you to sit on the ground and have your feet comfortably positioned.

Why would anyone want a hole blind? The pitblind for pronghorns has already been mentioned. It is cooler in a pitblind if you can stay out of the sun. Short vegetation may decree a hole blind in order to have adequate background cover. (Rattlesnakes like pitblinds, too, so you shouldn't leap blindly into your pronghorn pit.)

Ground blinds in whitetail country are safer than a tree stand in wet weather and more comfortable than a tree in cold weather.

Hole blinds are even more comfortable, providing you have thick enough padding to sit on, to prevent heat loss. Since you are closer to ground level, you will be more out of the wind. If you want supreme comfort, take a sleeping bag with you and pull it over your boots, legs and lower body. In larger hole blinds, much of your scent will be trapped in the hole.

Since you are at ground level, you will be at eyeball level with game—but any movements detected will be more natural to them because they are accustomed to seeing movement at ground level. The first animal I ever shot at with a bow was a whitetail doe which walked within eight paces of my hole blind. I hit her in the shoulder, the arrow bounced out and she took off. I shook for a week.

Hole blinds require forethought, especially in parts of the continent where soil freezes solid for many months. You dig hole blinds in the summer and fall, when the soil can be dug and when there is enough time for the odor of your activity and the freshly turned earth to dissipate.

Pronghorn pit blinds need the soil built up around in front and the sides of the pit quite often. Sagebrush cut and stuck in this soft soil completes the cover; it's also used to enhance the background when necessary. One of the most important tools for the successful bowhunting of pronghorns is a long-handled shovel with a sharp blade.

The hole blinds dug in deer country must have soil carried away and dumped someplace inconspicuous. A good hole blind will be unnoticeable, except possibly for a small circle of brush denser than the other brush.

A bowhunter I know used to make his hole blinds into living rooms. He dug them large, very large, carpeted the bottom, dug out a seat below ground level, had plenty of room to draw his bow and shoot the arrow *upward* at a close animal. He made one, though, on the end of a cornfield and got part of it too close to the area the farmer used to turn his tractor around. When the right rear tractor wheel fell into the hole blind, the tractor was as stuck as if in quicksand. That farmer was one of the angriest people to ever become angry, and justifiably so. Jim shoveled for an hour filling in his late, lamented hole blind.

The big problem with ground blinds is, of course, your scent line. It is right down there where game animals can get a strong whiff of it. Motion can be more easily detected at ground level too.

Ground blinds just might spice up your hunting if treestands are getting old. "Yessir, I got right down there amongst them. Would you believe it? Had that buck walk right in front of me at 15 paces. Never knew I was there. Danged exciting. Danged exciting, I tell ya."

Driving. Driving means the pushing of game from an area by moving hunters, called drivers, toward or past waiting hunters, called standers. Driving is often called pushing, for obvious reasons. Driving can include many or few people, it can be fast or slow, quiet or noisy. The most effective drives in bowhunting usually involve few people who progress relatively slowly and quietly. Hitting a running animal is difficult with any hunting tool but most difficult with bow and arrow.

In terrain well known to the hunters, one driver acting more as a stillhunter often can make extremely effective drives for one or two standers. A fellow I know in Wisconsin feels he can push whitetails to within 15 yards of where he wants them to go if he is careful. He isn't bragging either, just stating a fact on something he has done often.

Dog Hunting. Dog hunting is hunting with dogs and shooting the game with bow and arrow. No more, no less. It is used mostly by bear and cougar hunters.

The purpose of this chapter is to help you gain insight into the special needs and considerations of bowhunting and bowhunters.

Bowhunting's Requirements

The key to successful bowhunting is to get close and remain undetected, or if detected, unalarming enough that the animal ignores you after brief inspection or allows you to slowly draw, aim and get off a good shot.

Proper positioning has been talked about and will be noted more specifically in other chapters, mainly in the chapters on camouflage and clothing. It will be noted in more depth later in this chapter.

We must avoid skylining and silhouetting, even more than when gun hunting.

Our ears are used frequently, simply because most of our hunting is at close range. Noise is a natural factor in nature. Branches fall, acorns drop, the wind moves leaves and twigs, water tumbles and bubbles, rocks fall, animals scramble up trees, big game slips on rocks and cracks brush. Each species has its own vocal sounds, and some of them fight noisily. A carpet of fallen leaves rustles when walked on, especially after a hard frost. Then it's like walking on corn flakes.

Since we are using a short-range hunting tool, hearing the sounds of nature takes on added importance. Is that rustling behind us a squirrel or a deer? Most likely, if it sounds like a squirrel or grouse, it will be a deer, and vice versa. That's what it seems like, at least. Was that twig snapped by an animal within range, another hunter or something else?

We can make wrong noises and right noises. A softly snapped twig, if only one snap, is natural. Sounds like a feeding animal. Rattled antlers bring whitetails. Calls bring elk, turkeys, whitetails, muleys, foxes, coyotes and squirrels.

A metallic click, or a heavy clunk of bow against tree, or heavy twig snapping, or too many snaps, or twigs against clothing, or voices aren't so welcome in the wild world.

On the other hand, a sharp whistle sometimes stops an animal where you want to shoot at it. Any sharp, quick noise not repeated might work.

Friend of mine rattled in a buck one time by clicking one arrow across the other arrows in his bow quiver. The buck refused to come close enough, but my friend still felt he had accomplished something. He had. He thought quickly and improvised.

"I couldn't let the buck just walk past out of range," he said.

A handful of Missouri bowhunters like to brag of their ability to "whoa" a deer. They say it works more frequently than you would believe.

Their all-time favorite story is of the club member in a treestand having his afternoon quiet wait shattered by, "Whoa!" brief silence, then "Whoa. Damn you, I said Whoa!"

The shouter, another club member on stand at a nearby trail, later admitted that he had sort of lost control when the deer wouldn't listen. It did, however, run like hell when the guy shouted.

Now and then, we put our feeble noses to good use. Rutting elk have a strong odor which can be smelled some distance. Hogs have a distinctive odor. Javelina have a strong musk. Rutting whitetails sometimes can be smelled. Our nose can sometimes help in trailing wounded game; gut shots can be detected, sometimes, by the odor they emit.

No matter how or where we hunt, we need to be especially alert with our eyes. Motion is easily detected...the flick of a tail, the moved antler tip projecting above a log, the turning of an ear, the movement of a leg below the underbrush.

Using the right hunting technique for the situtation helps improve your odds for a successful hunt. Note that this bowhunter has his treestand strapped to his back, leaving his hands free to carry his bow and drag the deer.

Animal movement helps us particularly well when it is time to draw and shoot. Any animal in motion—us or otherwise—is less able to detect other motion when it itself is moving. Conversely, naturally, any animal sees other motion most easily when it is still. It is no accident that game animals wait until we walk past, then sneak or bust out the back way or stay right where they are.

This can get comical. One time a good whitetail buck was walking cautiously, but unalarmed, down a trail which would take it within 12 yards of my stand. Like an idiot, I shifted slightly on stand as it approached, instead of letting it walk past. I wanted to be ready to drill that dude...and I wanted to get an early glimpse of its headgear, hoping that it had headgear. It stopped, then turned ever so slowly and walked into the hazelbrush, leaving the distinct impression that it was thinking "If I don't move fast, maybe that thing in the tree won't see me." It was, of course, in full view, but it still moved slowly and carefully.

I shot right where I was looking. You cannot kill a deer when you hit its antler.

An animal can "jump the string," meaning that it avoids the arrow seemingly after you have launched it. This often is credited to the animal's fantastic vision or hearing and equally fantastic reflexes. Part of the animal's response may be because of those qualities, but I'm firmly convinced that the so-called jumping usually is triggered by an early part of the drawing motion rather than the sound of the string, or some sound we made, undetectable to our ears but fully noticed by the animal's ears. Besides, it has been conditioned by all it knows to take instant evasive action to survive.

Game often seems to squat to avoid an arrow. Again, its great reflexes help, but my belief is that the animal simply was reacting to the sound of the arrow passing harmlessly over its back. With our tension and everything happening so quickly, it is difficult to say what exactly caused what reaction.

Bowhunters sometimes ask whether they can smoke on stand. You can if you want, but why tempt fate? Smoke from a small wood fire on a cold day during gun hunting season has been know to pique an animal's curiosity and draw it in, so we give too much credit to the animal when we feel it can associate cigarette smoke with humans, unless there was some unknown prior encounter which helped the animal associate that odor with an alarming situation.

For my money, the motion a smoker makes with his arm and hand, putting the cigarette to his lips and removing it, is the alarm factor. This motion is so automatic for the smoker that he doesn't think of it.

Distance Barriers

Game has distance barriers. Whitetails sometimes seem to have roughly a 50-yard barrier. I am firmly convinced this is related to their highly developed sixth sense. How else could they have such a barrier when they aren't supposed to know we're around? This could, however, be the distance at which they exercise their natural caution on all items which arouse their suspicion. They obviously smell, hear and see effectively at much greater ranges than 50 yards, but why the hangup when one is approaching your stand?

If nothing happens to trigger an alarm, then the next barrier for the bowhunter is at 10-12 yards. At that distance, you're probably going to be wound as tight as a spring. There is little or no margin for error to begin with. When something happens, everything seems to explode in all directions at once.

The comfort zone, if it can be called that, generally occurs at 15-25 yards, longer than that in more open country. The animal is close enough but not too close. You still can maneuver if needed. You know you're accurate at that distance.

The bow may be a limited-range tool, but that doesn't mean an animal moving out of your range can simply be allowed to walk away. Freelance if you can. Follow it. At that point, there are no dumb moves, because you have nothing to lose and everything to gain. This is easiest in big, fairly open country, but can be done anywhere.

Ken Rose, an Ohio bowhunter, has taken a couple of deer by running after them. Whitetails like to stop and look back, once they have quickly put a short but seemingly safe distance between themselves and whatever startled them. When Ken startles a deer, he runs right down the trail after it.

"You have to be ready to draw and shoot the instant you see the deer," he notes, "but this goofy trick can be made to work."

Steve Gorr, a Washington bowhunter, dug a shallow trench in the middle of a hayfield after watching deer funnel to that spot through a shallow depression in the field. There was no other way to get at them, so he decided to let them come to him. He waited until he saw deer legs move past above the edge of his trench, then sat up and shot. All but one of the deer left the field immediately.

Arrows have been known to startle animals into moving closer to the hunter when the arrow which missed them landed with a thud on the side opposite the hunter. This is an instance where it pays to have a second arrow ready promptly.

Hunters have been known to walk, with the sun low and directly behind them and the wind quartering or in their face, right at animals. Nothing can see worth a darn when looking into the sun, and the hunters were able to get within good shooting range for a good shot.

Bowhunters make good use of natural funnels of all sorts...a neck of timber, a corner of a field, a brushy fencerow, a long shallow depression which may hide much of an animal's movement through heavy cover, and a lot of these funnels are not in heavy cover. They do, however, restrict animal movement to narrower paths, and that's what we as bowhunters need.

Animals don't just walk into bedding cover and plop down, either. Often they will circle downwind and come into their bedding area with the wind in their face. This obviously is the best defense in cover so thick not even they can see into it well. But they probably leave the bedding area into the wind or quartering it. Use this knowledge to position yourself properly according to the time of day—are the animals likely to be entering or leaving the bedding area when you set up near (but not too near) it?

We often forget that our eyes are positioned much farther above the ground than are most animal species. To get their view of the situation, kneel now and then. You might see a bedded animal, the legs of a motionless trophy waiting to let you walk by, or something else which helps.

We need to take advantage of barriers to movement, such as cliffs, lakes, openings, rivers, etc. Although not all lakes, rivers, openings, wet swamps, etc. are barriers to animal movement. Most of them swim well, and they aren't afraid to get their feet and legs wet.

Water is more of a barrier to us than to game. Check out wooded, brushy islands sometime and you will quickly see what I mean. The bowhunters who hunt islands a lot don't talk about it much, but they smile a lot to each other. Especially for photos of the game they took.

Remember that it is exciting to sit on the edge of a field or opening and watch the game which emerges to feed. But how often does that game emerge within good bow range? Seldom, and usually only young and dumber animals, and females. You just won't find many big busters in such open areas, and if you do see them there they often will be moving fast. They don't mind exposing themselves, as long as it is brief.

The best place for a bowhunter is back from the edge, back beyond the perimeter trail animals almost always have created parallel to openings. The smarter animals will be waiting back there for darkness to fall before feeling safe enough to move into the open to feed. In addition, their attention, or most of their attention, will be directed out toward the opening. If you're behind the area of thick cover, their attention will be directed away from you. That should offer the best shot.

Animals adapted to open terrain, of course, are just that—adapted. They use their eyes a lot and their speed.

Use stress on the animals to your advantage at times other than just when making drives. Turn the potential negative into a positive. Think. Be creative.

A friend of mine hunts for deer just off the edges of public

Hunting aggressively and being prepared can give you an edge over other bowhunters. These men are heading back into a swamp for a day's hunt. Sure, it's a little more work, but the result could be a trophy whitetail buck that has moved back in to get away from hunting pressure.

Don't forget about large grass or weed fields. It may look empty, but they can hold several species of game animals.

hunting areas on the opening day of pheasant season. His area doesn't have many pheasants; most of those which are in the area are pen-raised birds turned loose a week or so before the season. They usually are released in public hunting areas.

Pheasant season opens at noon, so Denny is on his stand at 10 a.m. near a low spot in a drainage ditch bordering the public land. Bird hunters start arriving around 11 a.m., followed closely by dogs running everywhere, car doors slamming, shouts, plenty of conversation.

Followed shortly after by unnoticed movements of deer sneaking out of the cover. Unnoticed, that is, to all but Dennis.

This same setup works during upland bird, small game and other seasons, too. Grouse hunters stomping through brambles and other heavy cover move deer everywhere.

Turn the absence of stress to your advantage. If an area you like is heavily hunted in the afternoons until quitting time, hunt it in the morning. Game will be moving more then, more than usual. If an area is hunted hard on weekends, hunt it during the week.

Hunters are famous for camping at Point A and driving to Point B to hunt, driving away from or right past good hunting pockets. This, of course, is part of the "grass is greener elsewhere" behavior syndrome. So these mid-range areas could pay off well for you.

Likewise, hunters prefer hunting ridgetops and valley bottoms, avoiding the steep-in-between area. So where do you suppose the game will be concentrated? Slopes can be rough going, but bowhunters need to move slowly and cautiously anyway. And if you are set up in there, the high and low hunters may bird-dog for you unintentionally.

Pockets of cover close to urban areas often aren't available to gun hunters, either through posting or concern for safety or both reasons. Often, though, they are available to bowhunters. Here, getting permission to hunt may be the most difficult part of a hunt.

"Pocket" conditions exist for all game, not just the whitetail deer which thinks it is a cottontail rabbit. Two years ago on a pronghorn hunt, my partners and I surprised several of these fleet animals holed up in little washouts that fingered off grassy draws. These pockets are especially good on windy days because they keep the animal out of the wind completely. On hot days, these spots can be cool, especially if there is bare soil.

Basically, there are few pockets of cover too small to hide game animals. We just *think* they are too small, and that is why we ignore them, which makes them safer for the game which hides there. In addition, some of these pockets may be difficult or impossible for a bowhunter to approach undetected.

Hunting Wet Weather Periods

Wet weather can be excellent for bowhunting. Blacktail deer areas, of course, in some areas of the Northwest and Alaska are almost always damp or wet, but other species can be hunted in wet weather.

Ground cover is quieter when wet. Sounds don't carry as far. Fog can obscure vision. Scents are more easily detected but don't move as far; there usually is less wind and the moist air holds it down. Animals don't like to get their inner ears wet, so they may turn them down, which reduces their hearing ability somewhat. They also tend to be more relaxed in wet weather, probably because there is less animal movement of all kinds then.

In my experience, a warm soft rain can offer outstanding hunting. Animals don't seem to mind it and often feed heavily then, especially if the weather is going to get worse.

You will need to pay special attention to your gear in wet weather. Waterproof feather fletching. Be sure your shooting glove or tab stays dry enough and doesn't crease. A creased tab gives a sloppy release. Your sight settings may change slightly, too, in wet weather. A 30-yard pin might now be a 29-yard or 28-yard pin. Atmospheric pressure causes some yardage loss. Water on fletching, arrow shafts, bow limbs, bow camo socks and bowstrings will add weight which slows everything down. A sloppy release will rob energy from the system, too.

In wet weather, keep your shots shorter and use a string tracker if possible or practical. Blood trails will be more difficult to see under these conditions and may be washed out completely.

Pay attention to your own physical needs, too. Stay as dry as possible, because you are not as good a hunter when you are wet and cold. You want to move too fast, to get warm or to get out of the lousy weather and back to a nice, warm camp.

Gray days usually see game moving more throughout the day. Since there is less light, they seem to relax. A gray day is a good time to spend the whole day hunting. Since you will be fully camouflaged, you will be more difficult to detect, but so will the game.

How The Wind Creates Pockets

Wind direction and speed can create pockets of good hunting for a bowhunter. Neither game nor hunters like to spend much time in a strong wind. Cold winds push us all into areas which are comfortable. Look in conifer thickets on windy days, the lee side of ridges and hills, low spots and swamps or tall grass. Tall grass may seem windy as the devil, but only when we stand upright. To see how game experiences it, lie down in tall grass. You'll find yourself in a snug nest. The wind won't be far over your head, but it *will* be over your head.

To figure out how best to hunt areas out of the wind, try to envision air flow as water flow. With that in mind, evaluate the terrain. Wind has eddy currents just like water. Some of those little pockets just below a ridge top or on the lee side of a hill or at the end of a valley can be almost impossible to bowhunt successfully because of eddying air currents and other swirling action.

Strong winds often make game animals nervous because they cannot hear well, and gusts of wind which rustle branches or leaves undoubtedly make an already-nervous animal more nervous. Have those brief rustlings occur randomly and it is easy to see why the animals have a hair trigger on their reactions.

Remember, though, that animals which live with constant wind are not bothered by it.

Air movement of even more importance to bowhunters is the thermal movement, that slight and often almost-undetectable movement of air created by changes in air temperature. Thermals exist everywhere, as far as I know. They are more pronounced where elevation and/or vegetative cover has a certain amount of variability, simply because it is easier for air to move on slopes, and vegetation variability means air won't heat or cool uniformly in a given area.

Remember, too, that vegetation causes air flow eddys just as surely as do hills and ridges. The eddys explain why you will see a light westward breeze, for instance, on the downwind side of heavy cover when the overhead winds are blowing strong to the east.

Forget the rule of thumb on thermals. That rule states that thermals blow up in the morning and down in the evening. Or is it the other way? I honestly cannot remember, because it is so patently designed to get a hunter in trouble that it is best ignored.

Thermals blow upslope only when the air at the bottom of the slope is warm enough to rise, and thermals blow downslope only when the air is cool enough to sink. Period.

In the morning, there will be downdraft thermals until the air warms enough to rise. Vegetative cover and degree of slope are the two main governing factors. These same factors influence the hour and minute when the air cools enough to cause it to sink.

A few years ago, on a Black Hills hunt in South Dakota, I sat comfortably downslope from a trail on a morning hunt because the heavy pine tree cover kept the surface area cool long into the morning. The downdraft thermal continued until 9 a.m., long after sunup.

In late afternoon, warm updraft thermals often continue until long after dark under some conditions. This is especially true during warmer times of the year.

So ignore the rule of thumb and position yourself according to the indicators in the area you hunt. Shift your position when the thermal shifts. Tie a light thread on your bow's upper limb tip or carry a squeeze bottle of white powder for a quick, handy checking system. Milkweed seeds with their parachutes work well, too, but they obviously aren't available everywhere. A pinch of dust might work, too. I like the light thread, because you can check it without moving. The thread needs to be extremely light to be effective, because a weak thermal won't move a stiffer thread.

It is often said that animals need three things—food, water and cover. Agreed. However, sometimes the water need is misinterpreted. In dry areas, waterholes often are paramount in importance and thus are excellent places to set up. In areas with more humid weather and generally more widespread water availability, setting up near water—except at a crossing—may be a waste of time. In such climates, animals often get all the water they need from their food. An animal eating grass on a dewy morning is going to get plenty of water, for instance. Bowhunters in such areas essentially ignore the water factor as it applies to an animal's internal physical health.

The rut is a known quantity relative to the quality of hunting available to bowhunters at that time. If you have to take vacation time to hunt then, providing the season is open, take vacation. Animals are less concerned for personal safety now than at any other time. They have their own tunnel vision now, and it is controlled by sex hormones. If an animal is going to act dumb, blatantly dumb, this is the time it will do so.

However, not all seasons are open during any given species' breeding season. This is especially a problem for deer hunters in some states with a fairly short bowhunting season, such as three weeks to a month.

What do you do then, if that is your problem? You want to maximize your hunting effectiveness, yet the hunting pressure may have pushed the deer into hiding.

First, obviously, be the best hunter you can be, as far as basic hunting knowledge and skills are concerned. Know the animal as well as possible.

Second, become more aggressive in your efforts. Western hunters are accustomed to the aggressiveness of looking for game, finding it, then hunting it. Eastern hunters are less aggressive in this manner, with the exception of driving game, because their hunting conditions are more conducive to a waiting game. Stillhunting for bear in this part of the country is a waste of time. Stillhunting for turkeys cannot be done successfully, to my knowledge. Stillhunting for deer can be done successfully, but this is one tough way to go after deer. Day in and day out, stands are the best.

You can, though, hunt aggressively while on stand. You can rattle antlers, use scents and lures, call or grunt, and use decoys. Just don't get your priorities out of whack. These aggressive elements are nothing more than aids to your basic hunting skills. They are not cures for what ails your basic hunting skills. The secret is: There is no secret. A good hunter will make these aggressive systems work much more successfully than will a poor hunter.

You can position your scent most any-where by taping a clothespin to a 35mm film canister filled with cotton. Saturate the cotton with the scent and pull it out above the rim so the air can circulate the scent.

When sex lures first caught on, countless bowhunters thought that all they had to do was set out an open bottle of lure and deer would come running. They forgot about the basics. Likewise with rattling, not just any noise will work.

So let's look at these in some depth.

Lures And Scents

Lures and scents can attract game animals—not just deer. Trappers obviously have know that since trapping began, and the use of lures for hunting came out of the trapping scene. There are food lures, sex lures, curiosity lures.

Food lures. Food lures in my experience, seldom work well as a lure because in attempting to fit in with the native foods animals are accustomed to eating in any given area, they are behind the eight ball from the start. Animals already know where the best food sources are; they have been frequenting those areas for months, days, years, centuries. They know what the best foods smell like and the concentrations of those natural food odors. One little spot of food lure set out by a hopeful hunter doesn't stand much chance. In fact, if the lure is used at the wrong time it could be an alarm scent. Who knows. But why take the chance?

Curiosity Lures. Curiosity lures usually are urine and sex gland based in a matrix. They might even have a food scent mixed in, but that is doubtful. These lures are designed simply to add the odor of an unknown animal to the area frequented by the animals you are hunting. Each animal has its own distinct scent which identifies it as that individual. So the new kid on the block might create curiosity among the animals living in the area, or might bring in a dominant animal to check it out and run it off or breed it.

Sex Lures. Sex lures are the urine and glandular lures made, or supposedly made, from female animals in estrus and from male animals of the species in full rut. Usually the lure is from the female only, and is supposed to consist solely of urine. Some lures have only male glands in them and are designed to appeal to the competitive instincts of actual breeding males in the area.

Masking Scents. Masking scents are not supposed to be lures. They are supposed to mask the human odor or any other odors which could be carried in by the hunter and possibly alarm an approaching animal. Some of these are urine based, such as fox, skunk, bobcat; others may be natural, such as pine, honeysuckle, acorn, earth. I believe that food scents could be included here, for they shouldn't be alarming and could serve to mask human or other odors.

Masking odors are designed to relax the animal, keep it from becoming suspicious.

Lure scents should *not* be put on your clothes or boots. You don't want to attract an animal's attention directly to you. Even if you want to use a lure scent as you walk to an area or through an area, put it on something other than pads on your boots.

The new drip systems are the best answer here. A small bag of scent hangs on your belt. The scent feeds out at a controlled rate, down a plastic tube and onto the ground at a rate slow enough to mimic the rate a female animal would drop her scent while moving when in estrus.

This system not only keeps the sex lure off you, it also drops the lure the proper way—the intensity remains constant and the freshness is the only variable. The idea is to have the freshness serve as a guide for any male of the species which is attracted to the scent, so it will follow the scent line in the direction of increasing freshness.

The problem with a footpad or separate drag bag is that the intensity is greatest when the trail is first begun, but the freshness is best at the opposite end of the trail.

There is no guarantee that an animal will automatically follow the trail in the desired direction, but you ought to set up that trail so the animal has the most factors prompting it to follow in the right direction.

The human animal tends to believe that if one of anything is good, two ought to be twice as good. Not so with scents and lures.

Too much scent can be unnatural and alarm the game animal or pique its curiosity, causing it to circle downwind and try to figure out the cause of it all. If you don't see that animal sneaking around—and chances are you won't—once it gets a whiff of you or sees a movement, it's gone. Gone for good, most likely.

This factor applies to lures and to masking scents. Too much sex lure is unnatural. Generally, put out one source of scent in a position ahead of you and on the side opposite that from which you shoot. Left handed shooters put the scent ahead and right; right handed shooters, ahead and left. The single source means you *know* where the animal will come to if it is attracted, and the left/right positioning means you need to move less as you draw. Placing the scent ahead of you keeps the animal's attention away from you. Do not put the scent directly upwind of you. Your scent and the lure can mix; besides, you don't want the animal coming past directly under you because that is a poor shot angle.

A lure scent simply allows you to hunt a 360-degree circle around your position.

A sex lure can be used to enhance an existing scrape or create a new scrape. Either way, the buck or bucks running that territory are led to believe they suddenly have competition.

Keep Yourself Clean

The best odor control you can use is a bar of unscented soap, and/or baking soda (which absorbs odors and is a rough element which helps scrape your skin), and a rough towel. Take a shower, or clean up as much as possible before you hunt. There are shampoos available with natural scents such as pine or acorn. Use one of them for your hair and your body.

Be sure you wash your groin area and armpits. They are the areas of most heat and thus cause most decomposition of dead skin cells, which creates BO and the heat does most to waft those lovely odors into the air.

If you don't have the desired soap and water, try a product called Tucks. These pads are handy.

Your hair is a repository for all sorts of odors. Keep it clean.

Wash your hunting clothes in unscented detergent, and add a drop of pine oil or a natural oil to the wash water. Don't use an anti-static fabric softener when you dry your hunting clothes; those items are scented. Hang your clothes outside to dry in the open air, if you wish.

Put your hunting clothes and boots in a plastic bag with some

The use of decoys can be an effective means of hunting certain game. This bowhunter is setting out a hen turkey decoy, to use with his turkey call in bringing in a gobbler.

crushed leaves, broken branches or other vegetation native to the area you will hunt. The escaping plant odors will give your clothes the right smell.

Don't wear your hunting boots everywhere, just when you hunt. Put them on when you leave your vehicle and remove them when you return.

Keeping yourself and your hunting clothes and boots clean do more than anything to mask the objectionable human odor. All a masking scent really should be asked to do is cover that little remaining scent or dilute it so the approaching animal believes you are farther away than you are.

Drenching each armpit with a bottle of masking scent isn't the way to go. It cannot replace cleanliness. The concentration of such an odor from overuse could backfire on you.

Other Tricks

Rattling. Rattling antlers attracts animals just like any other call, for it really is nothing other than a call, of sorts. Use good-sized antlers and keep them in good condition. Don't let them get too dry. Soak them in water, if needed; a light coat of linseed oil might be all that is needed.

Rattling *must* simulate a fight between two bucks. Toneless, uninspired clashing of antlers won't work. The sequence must be exactly as a natural fight would be *and* must have the pauses a natural fight would have. This silence is the time the actual fighting animals get their breath for another sortie.

Rattling works best when the buck:doe ratio is closer to even than when does greatly outnumber bucks. For obvious reasons— why fight when there is no need to?

Rattling works best before the peak of the rut and after the peak of the rut. So does bugling for elk. This is the time the males are on the prod but the females aren't yet ready or are past their peak interest. The rut is much longer than the breeding season; males are in rut much longer than females are receptive.

Grunting/calling. Calling is becoming more popular for whitetail deer as we learn more about it. It shouldn't be anything startling, because varmints have been called for eons, bull elk are bugled in, bull moose are called in, turkeys are called.

Decoys. Decoys are nothing new either; they're simply new to the hunting of whitetail deer.

There really isn't anything new. There are, however, a lot of things we don't know or have been too bound in our attitudes and thinking to see or figure out or apply.

This type of aggressive hunting, especially the use of calls, scents and rattling, have an extra benefit. They can pull animals out of property you cannot hunt onto land you have permission to hunt.

Don't Overdo It

Can these things be overdone? Of course. Bull elk shut up fast when their ears start ringing from all the bugling going on. Poor rattling technique can push bucks deeper into cover and make them more cautious. The incorrect use of scents and lures has already been noted. A point to note here: Vary the scents you use, so you don't pattern yourself for the game. The scent of fox mixed with a slight human odor could be alarming once, but almost certainly would be alarming if detected twice or more, for instance.

These elements can be used well in combination. Rattling can attract a buck from a couple of hundred yards, pulling it out of its bed in the cedars. When it moves close enough to get a whiff of lure or the sound of a grunt, it just might be reassured that all is what it suspects. The proper application of the combination may do the trick.

12

You Can't
Be Too Camouflaged

One question regarding camouflage never ceases to amaze me: "Do I have to...?"

No, you don't *have* to, but why go to all the other work and then take a chance on goofing it all up by neglecting a detail. The detail may seem minor, but it probably isn't. There is *no halfway* in camouflaging yourself and your hunting equipment. You cannot have too much camouflage.

Yes, we all have heard bowhunters say, "Ah, I don't bother with face camo" or "A camo jacket is enough camo on my body." This may explain why the speaker may not have done well in his hunting efforts.

But what about the times consistently successful bowhunters make such a statement? Are they discounting the value of camouflage? Not at all. What they are really saying is that other parts of their hunting efforts and camouflaging are effective enough that the thing they do not do is of no consequence. This is part of the "other" camo which will be discussed later. Those speakers are good hunters, darned good hunters. They can and do put themselves into situations where they get high-percentage shots at relaxed animals (or as relaxed as a wild prey species can be).

Let's take a close look at all aspects of camouflage, beginning with clothing, then equipment, then the "other" camo.

But before doing that, fix in your mind that the three items

most in need of camouflage—our face, our hands and our bow—
are the items most often overlooked. Why? Human nature, plus
failure to check all the details.

Clothing

Since all except those who are color blind see in four-color
images, we tend to value color highly and place too much value on
it in our camo clothing selection. However, color is not nearly as
important as pattern and light/dark tonal ratio. Camo clothing must
be matched to the background, whether it is conifers, deciduous
trees which have lost their leaves, brown grass, prairie, vegetation
with snow partially covering the ground, solid snow cover, or
whatever the situation.

The first time we buy camo clothes, we make darned sure we
get green camo for green surroundings, brown for brown
surroundings, and that's about it. There's nothing wrong with this,
but it is not the whole story.

It has been acceptably proven by researchers that animals *do*
see in four-color, apparently not as well as we do, but in four-color
just the same. This same research showed that animals were not
able to see in four-color as well as we are, needing bright sunlight
to see colors well and having much more rapid falloff in color
perception than do humans when viewing objects in partial
shadows or deep shadows or on gray days. (This does not apply to
turkeys, because it has been acceptably established by researchers
and by hunters that turkeys see very well in four-color. At times, it
seems like they also have X-ray vision and can see around trees
and bushes.)

So, to a degree, getting a color which matches the background
is all right. Movement, however, is the item animals key on most
heavily, especially when it happens too close to them and/or
appears threatening.

A good pattern is more important. Several patterns exist
today—World War II green-and-brown blotches, Tiger Stripe,
Vietnam, Trebark, Winona, Woodland, Desert, Snow, Leaf, etc.
All were designed with specific purposes in mind.

Another highly important factor exists or should exist within
the pattern. That is the light/dark tonal contrast. The greater the
contrast, the more effective the camouflage. This is why today's
camouflage patterns and colors have black in them and also
generally have lighter tans and greens than was available a few
years ago. Black against light tones provide maximum contrast.

The purpose of camouflage clothing is to help you blend in with your surroundings. There are many patterns and colors of camo, each designed for a specific use. This is a good example of light and dark tones necessary in a wooded/leafy environment.

It's as simple as that, yet I cannot emphasize it too much. The contrast must be great for the camouflage to be most effective. But the contrast also must fit within the surroundings and the backdrop.

Generally, a large pattern will be more effective than will a small pattern, because at medium and long ranges the smaller pattern will blend together and approach monochrome status. This especially happens when there is not enough contrast between light/dark tones. The old green/brown blotch pattern, commonly called the WWII pattern, is an example. It was good in its day, but other, newer patterns now surpass it. Take a look at much of the camo available 10 years ago and notice that very little of it had black as a color in the pattern and the pattern was mostly small blotches of green and brown which had little contrast. They generally were uniformly too dark.

The "deep, dark woods" isn't so deep or dark; in fact, look at how light the undersides of tree leaves are, the undersides of grasses, etc. In a breeze, with that vegetation moved around by wind, there is a considerable percentage of light tones visible, much more than our mind's eye wants to see simply because we have been trained to think and see otherwise, consciously and subconsciously. Our color vision overrides our tonal perception.

Patterns also are designed to match the surroundings in angles and directions. Tiger Stripe is vertical. The various bark patterns obviously were designed to hide a hunter most effectively when he is backgrounded by a tree trunk, hence the general light gray/black colors which closely match most tree trunks. The shape of the pattern also closely matches the bark of trees, and the contrast also closely approximates the tonal contrast of the bark itself.

Snow patterns are useful where you will encounter a good bit of snow and a mixed tonal background. Where there is lighter snow cover, I'd be more inclined to go with a brown camo pattern. A light tan or gray would work well here, too.

If you're planning a hunting trip out of your home territory, find out which camo patterns will work best in the new area. Green/brown/black might not work in the middle of a desert or a grassy prairie. In fact, light brown or tan work clothes with thin black lines randomly placed on them might work just fine in a grassy prairie setting.

Today's camouflage patterns generally are excellent. Manufacturers have put light tans, medium browns and black blacks into a pattern that thus has light, medium and dark tones. Same for light green, medium green and black.

Overall, I've found through photographing camouflage patterns and color combinations, a light/dark tonal range of 50/50 to 67/33 (dark to light) is an acceptable range.

To best evaluate any camouflage, look at it in poor light, which will most closely simulate your position in the woods. You're best hidden, like the predator you are, when you are back in the shadows or partial shadows. Color intensity is much less in poor light.

The flip side of this, of course, is to look at it in bright sunlight and note how difficult or easy it is to see the lighter tones. The tougher they are to see the better the camo, all other things being equal.

There's been disagreement on whether big game can see fluorescent orange. I've not formed an opinion, but I do know that a Colorado friend of mine said he has worn a solid orange cap, jacket and pants and sat motionless in a snowdrift while a herd of mule deer paraded by single file.

"All I can figure is that the orange must have looked pale to them and more or less blended me with the snow," he said. "Of course, I didn't move a muscle while they were in view, and that always is an important factor no matter what the other conditions."

My overall favorite camo pattern is brown-phase, with black, medium brown and light tan colors in big, irregular shapes. This color and pattern and tonal contrast will work in practically any cover anywhere.

Yellow can be a good camo color, too, as the light segment of the tonal contrast. Notice the quaking aspens in the West in the fall, or cottonwoods in prairie river bottoms, or maples in the Midwest or East, as examples. I wouldn't be surprised if it shows up in camo clothing patterns someday. Yellow and black would make an excellent combination.

When you're hunting in snow, you have to adapt to that background in general and your immediate background in particular. In some areas you might want almost all white, but in most areas you will want white or gray and dark brown or black. If you are hunting from the ground, you probably would want more white or gray than dark tones so you can hide effectively against irregular backgrounds or fairly open foreground, such as loosely spaced brush and/or grass. In a tree, darker combinations would most likely be best so you more closely match the tree itself.

If you want to test a pattern's light/dark contrast but cannot find a low light area, squint your eyes and look at it. This technique is used by artists to judge tones. Your eyes pick up less color intensity when mostly covered by eyelid—which really is the same as reducing light some other way. You may need to practice this a bit before it works satisfactorily.

All this camouflage pattern concern and care is of no value unless you apply it to clothing that is *soft and silent*. This means soft and silent in the woods, not when rubbed between thumb and forefinger when you're standing in a store examining it.

Poor fabric often has filler, making it seem heavier than it is when new and unwashed. This filler usually is nothing more than starch. Naturally, when this fabric is washed it will soften considerably, but it probably also will fade quite a bit. You are foolish to buy extremely inexpensive camouflage clothing, because the fabric won't have the necessary quality to wear well for many years, nor will it be likely to hold its color intensity for long. The wear-one-year-and-toss camo just doesn't cut it, and one of the big reasons is the fading. *Faded camo is no camo*! In fact, faded camo can make you stand out like a sore thumb. The only exception I can think of would be to use faded camo as prairie camo. Problem here is that cheap fabrics often become shiny when washed several times, so you might be right back where you started from.

Camouflaging Equipment And Yourself

Why do we so often pay closest attention to camouflaging the part of us which moves least—our body? Probably because that is the bulk of the camouflage situation. We need to have the bulk of our body camouflaged, but since it moves least it is easy to see why some bowhunters aren't overly concerned about whether they are wearing camo pants or a pair of brown, soft cotton jeans.

Our camo hat should have a brim, and the entire hat/brim unit must be soft. A hard brim would most likely interfere with the bowstring as you near full draw, and a hard surface is noisy. The brim must be large enough to shade the sun from your eyes but small enough that it won't block part of your vision when the bowstring presses against it.

Your face, how to hide it? Headnet, mask or camo cream. The choice is yours.

I seldom use camo cream because I get tired of its smearing on the turtleneck shirt I wear as the base layer of my clothing, and I get tired of the application and washing-off procedure. If you have sensitive skin, you might want to check the various creams to determine whether you can use them comfortably. I suggest you

A headnet can protect you from insects as well as cover your face and neck. One with a solid vision panel works best for seeing through.

stay away from the hard stick camo grease usually found at Army/Navy surplus stores. That stuff is so hard it will peel your skin off as you try to apply it.

The flip side of using camo cream is that it is cooler than a headnet or mask. In fact, some creams now on the market allow you to sweat right through them without washing off, and some contain insect repellent. That is a change for the better. On a South Carolina hunt in late August some years ago, I believe I set international records for fading. My camo grease didn't last much more than 10 minutes, and in that heat I didn't last a heck of a lot longer than that.

Creams also won't inhibit your vision (unless you get some in your eye while applying it, which burns and burns) as will a headnet or mask, so that is a point in their favor.

Headnets will keep out insects, which is a large factor in their favor when mosquitoes, black flies, no-see-ums and similar insanity-inducers are present. Headnets are easy to put on and remove, and there's no washing involved. However, headnets can be hot and difficult to see through. Most difficult to see through is camo mesh, for the light bouncing around between your eyes and the varying intensities of camo color can practically blind you.

The solution to this is to install a solid color mesh vision panel. The single, consistent tone makes viewing much easier. Dark green, charcoal or black mesh is easiest to see through. None of them are very good in extremely low light conditions. One addition will help—sewing a piece of black elastic to the upper corners of the vision panel, long enough to fit snugly around your head. This elastic will hold the vision panel closer to your eyes and improve vision.

Wearing a headnet *over* a short-brimmed camo hat will hold the headnet, except right where the elastic band and the vision panel are located, away from your head. This helps keep insects away. I'm sorry, but there is nothing I can suggest which will keep that lone mosquito from getting trapped inside your headnet, buzzing around and driving you batty. That comes with the territory.

A good method of keeping insects out is to fasten a strip of Velcro to the bottom of your headnet, then fasten the other half of the Velcro around the outside of your camo jacket and below the collar. Turn the collar up to help keep insects from your neck and seal the two Velcro strips together for a bug-proof connection. Tucking the headnet inside an upturned turtleneck also works well.

Those of us who wear glasses often feel trapped between a rock and a hard place, because we have the extra concern of keeping reflections from our lenses. Wearing a headnet helps quite a bit, but the best solution is to make darned sure we are positioned so sunlight cannot reflect from them. This is good hunting positioning anyway, back in the shadows.

A middle of the road alternative is a camo mask with elastic loops added top and bottom. The elastic fits around neck and head. I made mine large enough so I could pull it up to cover my glasses or lower it to the bridge of my nose and under my glasses. It obviously is not insect proof, but it works well and is easy to use. In low light, I simply slide it down so my glasses are uncovered, and I make sure I have my hat brim pulled down low over my eyes. This helps keep my glasses and eyes in shadow.

Whatever we use, it helps cover the light tones our skin possesses. Oil in our skin contributes to shininess, so simply washing our face can help dull the skin tones. We want to avoid having our face look like a reflective beacon as we scan the underbrush for approaching game.

Our hands move more than we think they do—changing position, scratching an itch, squashing a mosquito, etc. Much of this movement is unconscious, but it still exists and still is visible.

Camo grease or camo gloves solve the problem of visible hands. I shoot with a tab, so I simply cut a slit at the base of the appropriate finger and try to be coordinated enough to get glove, tab and finger together in the proper order and location.

Tape, sock and paint camo can be used on bow limbs. Tape works well but eventually comes off. Socks can catch on brush and adds weight to the bow, but are removable. Paint is permanent and easily applied.

A bow, shiny and new from the cardboard carton, is a sweetlooking thing. You almost hate to cover up those fancy colors and lines, but you had better do it. That bow is going to be moving at a tense time, and you don't want that motion attracting attention. You can do a plain or fancy camo job, but do it. I'm not much for splendor, so I just spray everything with flat black paint, let that dry then apply flat yellow paint as needed to break up the solid lines.

The bow quiver and bowsight bracket and mount also get painted.

Earlier I said that there is no way to have too much camouflage, but I'm modifying that here. I can accept camo arrow shafts, but not dark or camo fletching. As a responsible bowhunter, you have an overriding need to see your arrow when it hits the animal to identify the location and type of hit as much as possible, which is the key to your subsequent trailing and tracking efforts.

Some bowhunters use orange fletches, or combinations with orange as one of the colors. I use orange and white, and I use orange arrows. Once in a great while the orange shafts and light fletching might get an animal's attention, but only if you move wrong—and by then you should be drawing when the animal cannot become alarmed or chances are darned small it will be alarmed.

The adhesive strips of bright fur or fake fur applied to the shaft just ahead of the nock are fine hit identification aids, and they won't give away your position.

The "Other" Camo

There are several camo systems. We just aren't conditioned to think of them as such. Many are part of other hunting planning, positioning and efforts but still are camouflage. Consistently successful bowhunting means paying attention to details, and that is what these are...details.

Fully effective camouflage is a *system* of preparation and positioning which breaks up our physical outline, makes our movement on stand or during the stalk unnoticeable or unalarming, renders us and our gear silent, and holds our body odors and potentially alarming odors on clothes and boots to a tolerable minimum.

Camouflage clothing does most of its work at long and medium distances. Even if you are in a treestand 12 feet off the ground, at those distances you will still be within the game animal's field of vision. Now that we have taught deer to look up, we will be well within their frame of reference, too.

At *close range* other factors shift to highest importance. At close range, *silence*, *no alarming odor* and *no alarming motion* are three critical elements.

Not all game animals have all three defense systems—eyes, ears, nose—equally well developed, but those systems exist. A common statement among skilled deer hunters is, "You need to fool two of the deer's three defenses for consistent success, one of which must be the nose. Fooling only one sense may reduce the animal's concern and not alarm it, or it might increase the concern or pique its curiosity. It may want to know more about whatever caught its attention, unless its nose was so full of human scent it knew all it needed to know right then."

Here, in no particular order, are items to keep in mind. All are important, and when you think of them and act upon them as part of your total camouflage efforts your hunting skills will increase.

Keeping warm is an important part of total camouflage. We'll examine that more closely in the next chapter, but an item worth

Don't forget the most obvious. Fresh lumber in a woods is hardly camo, not until it's painted.

noting here is that your face mask, tucked under your collar or inside your shirt, helps keep the wind from your neck. Turn up your collar or zip your sweater up around it and you will be warmer, sit quieter, sit longer.

Rubber boots keep your foot scent in and shed other scents well, except for gas, oil and other chemical odors which shouldn't be permitted to be near your footgear anyway. Wear them as much as you can.

Stand positioning in the very best location will or should set you up so you are out of the animal's line of view as it approaches and passes. Placing a treestand on the side of the tree opposite from the expected approach of the game animal can hide you better, let you be in the best shooting position as the animal walks past and is looking beyond you. You can position yourself too close to a trail and not leave yourself any margin for error...and at the same time be so close that you're a nervous wreck when the game arrives.

Shiny objects such as rings, belt buckles, metal snaps and zippers, watchbands and faces, buttons, parts of the bow or accessories, bare metal on a treestand, eyeglass frames and the lenses themselves...all of these can twinkle and catch an animal's attention.

Equipment noise as you draw the bow, or a squeaky treestand as you shift position, or a clicking chain against framework-...won't do you any good. Carpeting on the treestand platform prevents noise. A plastic bag over that platform keeps snow and ice from it, to be dumped off when you climb into the stand.

Comfort. Did you remove that knob on the branch you are seated on, the one which is only the size of an acorn now but will be the size of a grapefruit after it has pressed into a cheek for half an hour. Small pockets sewn on the knees of your camo pants will hold the bow's lower limb tip and take weight off your muscles.

If you hang your bow to relieve muscle strain, hang it above you or level with your hand. You want to avoid raising the bow, because upward movements in the wild generally are movements of alarm—the frightened squirrel going up a tree, a flushed grouse. Downward movements are reassuring or neutral—falling leaves, a bird landing to feed, a squirrel coming down the tree, ripe nuts falling.

A direct stare at an animal can trigger its sixth sense, and it will look right at you for no apparent reason. Watch it out of the corner of an eye until you want to look directly at it to aim well.

The flip side of this, of course, is that you want to watch the approaching animal as much as you can, noting whether it is tense or relaxed. If you have done your homework, you will know what the animal is saying through body language. You then will know better when to move and when not to move.

To minimize movement at the moment of truth, get as close as possible to drawing early in the sequence. If you have your bow up, bow arm extended, sight following the animal...at the right time, all you need to do is draw, aim and release. The only motion is drawing your bow, and that is accomplished quickly.

Sometimes it is possible to draw, aim and release a good shot at an animal which sees you do it. That movement will need to be done slowly and smoothly, but now and then it can be done successfully. After all, that animal isn't supposed to know that's you about to launch a flying knife; all it is supposed to compute is a motion which caught its attention and might need further evaluation.

Wind Direction should be an obvious concern, too, but it sometimes isn't. Remember that nothing can replace or override basic hunting skills. Scents, calls and such are nothing more than aids to your basic hunting skills. They are not magic answers, nor are there any big secrets—there are just things we haven't learned yet or ignore when they are practically screaming at us to pay attention. So you pay attention to details and don't tempt fate.

After all, we as hunters are just as important a portion of the total hunting equation as are the game animals. Through the proper use of all aspects of camouflage, we will disappear in the woods.

13

Clothing
For The Bowhunter

The business world tells us we're supposed to dress for success. The same is true in bowhunting, probably even more so.

The game animal is one part of the bowhunt. Our equipment is another. We are the third. A regular triumvirate, sort of an unholy trinity.

Which part do we pay the least attention to? Ourselves. This is natural, because all our thoughts and enthusiasm are directed outward. We want to have good equipment, and we want to get out there and hunt.

There's plenty of time later to think about the fact that we are frozen solid, that our feet are numb, that our heavy clothing is so tight we can't even draw smoothly. Or that we took off in such a rush that we forgot the mosquito repellent, or forgot to check the canteen for water. Or that the raincoat would have been nicer on our body than back at camp during that cloudburst. Or that the first aid kit should have been in our pack instead of the back of the truck. Or one of a dozen inconveniences.

A lot of times these overlooked details are no more than inconveniences, affecting very little. But they can be much more than that, especially because bowhunting many times is a solitary sport where no one knows for sure where we are, or because we might be in big country far from help. Mother Nature is not benevolent, nor is she forgiving.

You know why water often is such a great barrier to our hunting efforts? Because we don't think far enough ahead to take with us boots of the right length. A nine-inch boot isn't much good when the water is 10 inches deep.

Yet watery terrain can be tremendous hunting — as soon as the mosquitos slack off — simply because hardly anyone thinks to bring long enough boots, or waders if they're needed, to enable them to get back in the sloshy stuff. With a little pressure, guess where the game goes? You got it.

A friend of mine hunts whitetails only in swamps, *way* back in those swamps near his cabin. The only hunters he sees all season long are those in his own group.

"The rut is interesting," Lou says. "Those bucks feel so secure back in there on the sand islands and among the reeds that they won't leave. The does move back in there during the rut. I almost envy those bucks....except for the ones we shoot."

Another friend of mine used to fill half of his station wagon with footgear for a weekend. He took tennies, leather boots, pacs, rubber knee boots, hip boots and extras of each just in case.

His wife lets him pack his own gear. "I'm staying out of that," she said. "I counted one time, and he had 10 pairs of footgear with him. Imelda Marcos could have taken lessons from him."

Crazy? Not at all.

Every part of the country likes to brag/complain that "If you don't like our weather, just stick around five minutes and you'll get something else." From my experience, the championship in this arena has to go the Western prairie country, where you can be sitting in hot sunshine one minute and half drowned by a cloudburst the next. You're miserable if you didn't bring a raincoat. The only consolation is that you will dry off soon.

Are you prepared to hunt wet country like the Pacific Northwest or Alaska? Dampness equates with misery if you're not well prepared....and sometimes even when you *are* well prepared. I have not yet experienced an Alaskan fogging-in, but I hear that it is a humdinger. Physically and psychologically.

A couple of years ago, I hunted deer in Alabama in late January. The day I left Alabama for my Wisconsin home, it was five degrees colder in Alabama than at home. Not only did my feet freeze because I had taken only leather boots instead of pacs, I doubly froze because I wasn't psychologically ready for those temperatures in Alabama.

There is nothing, however, that can compare to December

hunting for whitetails in North Dakota, where stopping the chilling effects of the wind is the main concern. The right type of clothes and the right kind of clothes and the right fit of clothes are important to comfort, hunting ability and personal health.

The first time I tried mountain country hunting, I brought a pair of mountain boots — that's what the advertisement called them — and ran in them all summer to get them and me in shape. They weighed about 80 pounds each, it seemed, and were far too stiff. They were mountain *climbing* boots, not hunting boots.

There is no law which says you need heavy boots just because you're at a higher elevation. Regular boots and tennies work just fine in most spots. Besides, those deep lugs on the stiff boots catch on rocks and twist your ankle half around, and they snag on little stones which kick down the hillside and upset the wildlife as well as you. Higher up, I know, sheep and goats are accustomed to rockslides and individual rocks falling. It is a different story down in mule deer country.

The gist of all this is simple: An uncomfortable hunter is a poor hunter. Second-guessing and impatience come easy when you are overheated and exhausted, or wet and cold, or dry but frozen stiff, or even worse, wet or damp and seemingly frozen stiff. The grass looks greener someplace else, so you begin fidgeting. Now you're going to be more easily noticed by game animals.

There's the safety factor, too. Extreme heat or extreme cold can be dangerous. Overexertion in otherwise-acceptable temperatures can create the onset of hypothermia or hyperthermia when there should be no danger.

When you get uncomfortable and/or tired, you become less careful. That can lead to accidents, and carrying sharp-bladed equipment around in rough country, or crossing fences and climbing trees with the same gear, or just traveling through rough country, certainly offers plenty of opportunity for accidents.

I particularly remember a javelina hunt in Arizona some years ago. All vegetation there seems to have thorns large or small. You watch where you step and you watch where you put your hands. When you're fresh, avoiding the thorns is no big problem. However, returning exhausted the first evening, I began letting brush slide off me like I might in my native Midwest. That is, I assumed it would slide. A couple of painful, stabbing encounters taught me a memorable lesson.

Cold weather is the most common problem, but it sure isn't an exclusive. You can get awfully dehydrated in a pit blind waiting

Wearing the right kind of clothing from head to foot, can make the difference on whether you hunt well or hunt poorly. Dress for the weather and terrain you will be in. Proper fitting, layered clothing is the best—the only—way to go. This way you can make adjustments according to your activities.

for pronghorn at a waterhole. You can get bitten beyond belief in a warm woods if you don't have adequate protection from insects. You can suffer heatstroke and get fried to a crisp if you move too much too fast in hot weather and without proper skin care and clothing.

You can sabotage yourself through inexperience in a new area. "Slightly turned around" can elevate to "*lost*" in a hurry, which often leads to panic and increased danger. For my money, the "smaller" country of the Midwest, East and South can be much more dangerous in this regard than big mountain country, because the flatter terrain has fewer distinguishing landmarks. Add a cloud cover and you can have big problems. One acre of hunting territory looks like the next. Step 20 yards into an alder swamp and you'll see exactly what I mean.

Get all sweated up and you can be in big trouble, in hot or cold weather. Evaporating perspiration can lead to super-cooling of your body. That can remove body core heat, and then you are in big trouble. Especially if you don't recognize the symptoms of approaching danger.

As bowhunters, we may be particularly susceptible to such problems at times because we might have a burst of energy used in getting to a particular place, then we become totally inactive for several hours. We can get too much, then too little heat creation/retention if we're not careful. Those are extremes, but we do them.

Watching how we exert ourselves is basic, or should be basic. For instance, if we leave camp for our stand 15 minutes earlier than necessary, we can walk slower, get less heated, create less perspiration, radiate less body odor *and* perspiration, which could later be a chilly problem.

The fact that slow movement is important in finding game animals before they find us when scouting, stillhunting or stalking should have carryover benefits, and it can. Those benefits are not automatic, however.

When we go to a stand, or are headed anywhere, we need to dress lighter and be able to get rid of body heat and moisture easily and quickly. That's when a day pack comes in especially handy for carrying extra layers of clothes. As we walk, if we're not hunting, we might want to remove our hat because 46 to 48 percent of all body heat is lost from our head and neck. Blood vessels are close to the skin in these areas so they radiate heat easily. Zipper turtlenecks are excellent in cold weather because the zipper allows adjustment for heat loss or retention and moisture venting.

Our clothing must be made of the right material for the weather and our activity. In warm weather, cotton might be fine because it holds moisture and thus may cool you comfortably as perspiration evaporates. In cold weather, cotton is a killer for the same water-retention factor. Cotton socks can be especially uncomfortable even when just slightly damp, because wet feet become cold feet, and our feet are the first things to chill on our body, generally, simply because they're the furthest from our body core and are not as essential to survival as is the body core. When heat creation is reduced, feet and hands are the first to cool.

Conversely, then, dry feet can make you feel more comfortable even when other parts of you might be damp or chilled. That's why it's a good idea to keep a dry pair of socks in your pack on day-long hunts away from camp, especially if your feet perspire a lot. If you don't have a spare pair of dry socks to change into in the afternoon, take off the socks you're wearing and rub your feet dry. The rubbing also will relax and warm your feet.

Polypropylene is excellent because it wicks moisture away from your body. Some people feel that this material holds perspiration odors even after washing, but I have not found that to be true. Polypropylene underwear generally is made in three thicknesses for different degrees of coldness and/or activity.

Polypro/wool combinations are becoming more common. They are excellent, too, unless you are allergic to wool.

I cannot comment on silk because I've never worn it, but people have told me they wore it as long underwear and it worked well.

Fishnet underwear is excellent, because its loose mesh creates the necessary air pockets for best insulation. In fact, I have found it to be too hot when worn while doing a lot of moving. Never kneel or sit on a hard surface when wearing this stuff, unless you want a waffle weave pattern imbedded painfully in your hide.

Panty hose help keep you warm. Don't chortle; pro football teams wear nylons in cold weather.

No matter what you wear or what it is made of, use the layering plan so you have more adaptability to your activity level and to the weather. The key item here is to be certain you increase the size of the garment every, say, second or third garment so the inner layers are not constricted.

Clothes must not be baggy or too tight. Bagginess can catch on brush or on a bowstring. Extreme tightness is worse, for it prevents

Wool slash-palm camo mittens will keep your hands and fingers warm in cold weather, and lets you have full sensitivity on the bowstring when it's needed.

dead air space between layers, and trapped air is an excellent insulator. Tightness also restricts movement. Be sure, too, that sleeves and waist are long enough on shirts, sweaters and jackets. This helps keep you covered and warm when you raise your arms to draw the bow.

Bib overalls and coveralls can be excellent because they cover your kidney area (critical to keeping warm and comfortable), have fewer air vents and don't restrict clothing movement at your waist, such as when you have to turn, draw and shoot. Suspenders ought to replace belts on pants so there is better air flow from bottom to top of your body, and less constriction of clothing.

Something as simple as sticking your pants cuffs inside your boots will help retain heat and keep you more comfortable. A ski mask will cover your head and neck, with only your eyes and/or eyes, nose and mouth exposed. You will be much warmer with your neck covered, even if it is just an upturned collar keeping the wind off.

When you buy footgear, be sure to buy it large enough. Felt pacs and a couple pairs of socks, plus a removable inner sole (commercially made or homemade from corrugated cardboard) will keep feet comfortable. The more heat loss barriers you can put between the soles of your feet and the ground, the better off you will be.

Rubber boots are great for shedding scent and outside moisture, but they can be extremely cold on the inside. If you want to wear rubber boots instead of rubber/leather pacs in cold weather, buy them large enough so you can place felt pacs inside them, plus a pair or two of socks. This combination will find your socks getting wet, and maybe even your pacs, but with dry spares you can keep you feet dry and warm.

Wool is an excellent outer layer because snow and ice don't cling to it. If I were hunting in generally damp, cool or cold conditions, I'd want as much wool as I could get.

The wind makes a big difference, too. Get out of the wind and you will instantly be warmer. I have a light windbreaker of the old "wet look" style which is ideal between a couple layers of clothes. The wet look was created by running a hot iron over nylon woven material, which softened it and thus unintentionally quieted it. The tight weave stops the wind, but it still is nylon and thus not silent. That's why it goes between layers of quieter material.

Bowhunters have worried about the potentially alarming odor (to wild game) of handwarmers. I think that was an inflated concern, but that may be of no concern soon. Products such as the Re-Heater, which is self-contained, don't give off odor. If you are really cold, put the handwarmer in a small bag and suspend it on a string down your back between layers of clothing. I've also seen guys tape a heater to the top of each boot for toe warmth.

What do you do about fogged glasses? I wish I knew. There is supposed to be a new plastic lens material on the market which won't frost up, made by Permaclear of Minneapolis, Minnesota. I haven't tried it yet, but I will.

One other thing: If you ever see a guy in a treestand with heavy material fastened to the stand's platform and the top of that material held up by suspenders, don't laugh. That might be me, and I *will* be comfortable. Beats taking a sleeping bag to the stand, which has been done. Besides, you can put all sorts of stuff at the bottom of that attached bag, move your hands and feet inside it, and all will be hidden from view.

In sum, there *is* a time to get selfish in your bowhunting efforts. That time is when you need to pay attention to the possible personal dangers, and when temperature extremes could make you so uncomfortable they rob you of your ability to hunt as well as you should. The game can go its merry way and frustrate your hunting efforts, but when it comes to succeeding in the physical comfort area, look no further than the mirror to see who is responsible. It is an important responsibility, for you are part of the total hunting equation.

14

Trailing Tips
To Save Your Game

Everything up to this moment has happened right because you paid attention to detail. OK, maybe a little luck entered, too, but we'll all accept that. Now, though, with tracking and trailing, the attention to detail really shifts into high gear.

I don't want to say this is where the work begins, because good tracking/trailing isn't work. It is demanding; it must be meticulous, methodical, careful, persistent and thorough. But it is not work. In fact, the satisfaction gained from a good tracking/trailing job is hard to beat. This effort is a separate challenge, one which you must respond to with all your skills and efforts.

Most bowhunters, once they have done enough tracking/trailing to feel reasonably good at it, get a special thrill out of this part of the total hunting effort. It is a feeling of "We almost have success in our hands. Let's not let it slip away from us."

There's more, too, for the instant you put an arrow into an animal, you assume a heavy responsibility to that animal to do all you can to be sure it is recovered. True, nothing in nature goes to waste, but that isn't the point. When a wounded animal is lost, something is taken from the joy and satisfaction of your hunting effort. An incompleteness exists, as well as a sense of loss and remorse.

You also have a responsibility to yourself to give it your best effort. The sport of bowhunting—all hunting, really—always deserves your best effort.

It is important to understand that not every animal hit with an arrow is "lost," in the sense of mortally lost. Wild animals have an incredible physiological defense system. They can recover, and recover well, from injuries which would finish a human in very short order. Additionally, a superficial hit is a superficial hit. There's no other way to look at it.

So don't make the mistake of thinking that every animal hit with an arrow and not recovered has run over the hill and died. You would only be adding to the misconception if you believed and talked that way.

Every once in a while a gun hunter will rail at bowhunters and bowhunting about supposed inefficiencies and cruelties when an animal is taken which is found to have, upon butchering, a broadhead or broadhead and part of an arrow shaft, somewhere in its body. The animal was healthy or the hunter wouldn't have taken it or tagged it after taking it. That fact gets conveniently overlooked.

The animal's internal defense system simply forms a hard covering around the foreign object and walls it off, isolates it. The irritant ceases to exist, as far as the animal's body is concerned.

The pain factor of an arrow? Baloney, mostly. Nerve endings exist only in a couple of layers at the skin. There or when physical function is affected—such as with a broken bone—is the only place pain will be felt. There are no nerve endings internally, so a broadhead moving around inside does not cause pain.

This knowledge won't help you find the animal, but it is good to know.

Read The Shot & The Animal

Now let's get you on stand. You have just hit an animal with an arrow. Now what?

Well, if you saw the animal go down, go over and tag it and dress it out. There's not a hell of a lot of sense in waiting "X" minutes as is so often written, if you can see the animal laying there stone dead. It needs to be dressed as soon as possible anyway.

A bowhunting friend mentioned once that he thought the animal lost control of its tail first. He was speaking of whitetail deer, which have a highly visible tail, especially when lifted, when he noted "If you see a big swirl of white, there's an awfully good chance the deer will be down just a few yards away. I'm not saying that happens every time, but I've seen it happen often enough to believe that the swirling tail is more than coincidence.''

Since then I've tried to remember that when watching a whitetail run off with my arrow, and I agree that once in a while it happens, not always but enough to be more than coincidence.

The instant you release, try to fix in your mind the *exact* position of the animal because you will need to check that spot later.

Watch the animal closely as it moves away. If the arrow is visible, try to pinpoint its exact position, angle into the animal and amount of penetration. Use binoculars if you can get them to your eyes quickly enough because they will help you get a better look. Watch for other signs, too, especially if you cannot see the arrow. (Sometimes the arrow can give a bit of a false reading. It can bounce back some if it strikes bone on the far side of the animal; escaping blood, out the entry wound, also can push the arrow back some.)

Does the animal hump its back and/or have its tail clamped tightly against its rear? This can indicate a gut shot. If you see the animal lie down—not fall down—you can be sure it is gut shot.

Rifle hunters are accustomed to noting that heart shot animals, especially deer, sometimes leap straight up, then dash off. Sometimes this happens with an arrow through the heart, too. Usually, though, the animal just wants to get out of there, which is a normal response to being startled. Bear will sometimes fight the arrow or bite at the wound before taking off.

Can you see blood anywhere on the animal? The first pronghorn I shot had a big red rose on its side before it even raised its muzzle from the water it was drinking. The next one I shot, hit almost in the same place (through the middle of the lungs), had no sign of blood at all on the entry side.

Watch the tail, as noted earlier. I've seen mortally wounded whitetails run off with tail down; I've seen others, also mortally wounded, run off with tail up and bobbing back and forth like it usually does when the animal is only mildly alarmed but untouched. So the tail is not a fail-safe indicator, but sometimes it can tell you something.

Don't assume that just because an animal runs into a sapling or bush it is losing control. When an animal leaves the area, especially a big animal, it is more concerned about getting out of there than watching where it is going. When an elk runs off, you would think at times that the entire forest is falling. A bear doesn't do a bad job as a bulldozer either.

There simply are many variables in responses, which is all the more reason to watch carefully and assume little. For instance, some hard hit animals will seem to run lower to the ground than poorly hit or missed animals. On the other hand, a startled animal often will run closer to the ground than usual as it leaves the area. I think this is more of a defense posture than an indication of a hard hit.

I once kicked a cow elk out of her bed in some black timber, and that elk never did fully straighten its legs as it scrambled out of there. I've seen whitetails leave their bed in the same manner. It is almost as if they are squatting with all four legs to lower their profile.

I've seen hard hit animals act unhit, and missed animals act as if they were hit.

Use your ears, too, especially if you cannot see the arrow's flight to the animal as well as you want. A sharp crack could be a bone hit or a sapling hit. A ribcage hit can be more of a plunking sound. A gut shot can be a softer plunking sound. A sound like ripping silk can be a muscle hit, or it can be the sound of skin being sliced on any hit. A hit in a heavy muscle only can be a more solid sound, because it is hitting something more solid than the internal organs. An arrow which just creases the animal usually won't make any sound, unless, for instance, the broadhead touches bone.

You probably will be more attuned to sounds on longer shots because the arrow will be more difficult to watch at a longer distance and you will have more time to listen as well as watch. On the other hand, everything happens so fast on close shots that getting a good view of the arrow is tough.

With the hit, note exactly where the animal moves out of view, and listen more. An arrow clattering against bushes and saplings and trees usually is easy to hear. Sometimes, too, you can hear the animal fall. This sound usually is different from the standard movement sounds which fade in the distance.

Reading The Hit Area

Now that the animal is out of sight, what next? If you are on the ground, note exactly where you are standing. Common instruction is to wait an appropriate length of time, depending upon your analysis of the type of hit and the time needed for it to be fatal. Another benefit of waiting occurs with a species that is likely to dash out of sight when spooked, whether wounded or not, then

A couple drops of blood on the water plus a smear on the edge of a reed every few feet was all the sign that was left on this trail by a hit whitetail.

circle back to see what spooked it. Also, a wounded animal sometimes will circle and attempt to get back to some place it feels comfortable. Either way, you may get a second shot. (You also may get a second shot on a missed animal that doesn't spook.) I hunted black bears with a guy one time who shot a bear at the bait, then watched it run in a 40-yard loop, dash back over the bait and right under his treestand, then collapse 15 or so yards past his stand.

However, I don't completely buy the "wait no matter what" concept. What's wrong with waiting to see if the animal intends to circle, or immediately moving downwind to outfox it if you believe it may circle back, and then in a few minutes, after marking your shooting position if you shot from the ground on a stalk or stillhunt effort and don't have the obvious treestand or ground blind to note your position, going to the place the animal was hit? You can make a careful, quiet check of that area, maybe follow the trail a bit for additional sign, and then assess whatever information you pick up to decide what to do. You obviously don't want to move in on the animal too closely or too quickly, but on the other hand additional information picked up may alter or correct your first impressions.

First things to look for are your arrow, hair, blood and tracks. If there is no other sign, there may be tracks to follow.

If you cannot find your arrow, continue your search as if you hit the animal. Always assume you hit the animal, until *proven* otherwise, if you cannot find your arrow. One of the worst statements which can be made is, after a cursory check, to say, "Let's go. There's nothing here, and there are more animals out here anyway."

That statement makes a veteran hunter want to administer a spanking—because the statement is irresponsible and childish.

A found arrow may be clean, which will be disappointing, but a clean miss can be a relief compared to knowing you have a poor hit. The arrow may be covered with pinkish blood and have air bubbles in the blood, or circles indicating where bubbles existed. These bubbles indicate a lung hit, with the bubbles created by air in the lungs.

Bright blood with no bubbles can indicate an arterial hit. If there is a lot of it, the animal should be dead not far away. Arteries carry a lot of blood under pressure, so when cut they shoot out large quantities. Femoral and carotid artery hits are good examples.

Vein blood usually is darker and in less quantity. Most leg hits are an example of this. The hit shows much blood at first, but the trail becomes progressively faint and then quits. Arteries take oxygen-rich blood *from* the heart to all parts of the body; veins take oxygen-depleted blood (which is darker) from the body back *to* the heart. Seems like small vein blood clots quicker because there is less pressure and less quantity. Large veins won't clot as quickly.

Blood circulation in the neck is a good example of blood color. The carotid artery carries bright red blood to the head, while the jugular vein carries dark red blood from the head back to the heart.

A paunch hit should leave bits of partially digested food from the stomach or intestine on the arrow. There may also be traces of dark blood from veins or bright blood from the pyloric artery (low in the belly cavity) or aortic artery (high in the belly cavity, just below the spine). Dark liver blood could also be there. Lacy belly fat, which forms outside and around the stomach and intestines could also have caught on the arrow or fletching.

Harder fat caught in the broadhead or smeared on the arrow shaft usually indicate a brisket hit or a very high (above the loins) back hit. But sure to check fat texture.

Check for hair on the broadhead, arrow and fletching. The type of hair in color, length, straightness and size could greatly help identify the hit. Examine the pelt of an animal sometime and pay close attention to the wide variety of hair types and their locations.

Look on the ground for hair which has been clipped from the body by the broadhead.

Mark the place the animal was standing when hit. If you were in a treestand when you shot, be certain you can find the hit site. The terrain may look a bit different from ground level, so you may have some difficulty pinpointing the hit site.

Before taking the trail, let's go back to the waiting time. The generally-accepted 30 minutes is a good guideline for lung/heart-/liver hits. With gut shots, an eight-hour wait is not too long and 12 hours is even better, when no major arteries or other organs are hit. The paunch has plenty of blood vessels, but they are small and require time to bleed enough to affect the animal's functions. This is where a check of the trail for a short distance might give you reason to move on the animal sooner, such as if you find indications of a liver hit or one of the arteries. A gut shot animal usually feels sick instantly and wants nothing more than to lie down. It still has full strength, however, so following it too soon most likely will spook it into wild flight. There will be a poor trail or no trial, and that too often means a lost animal.

The accepted theory on leg hits, especially solid ham hits, is to trail immediately "to keep the wound open and bleeding." I'm not so sure about that.

A lot depends upon how sharp your broadhead was. A dull broadhead or one with a feather edge will send more alarm bells to the animal's system, triggering more platelet release, than will a slickly sharp, broadhead. The thromboplastin in these platelets, not the platelets themselves, actually begins the chemical reaction which begins the clotting process. The dull or feather-edge blade will not penetrate as far as the slickly sharp blade, and it will do less cutting even if it could penetrate as far. Also, blood vessels suffer spasms when traumatized. The rougher the trauma (such as from a dull blade), the more the spasms. These spasms aid platelets in thromboplastin release, which naturally speeds up clotting.

In a nutshell, the wound caused by a dull or feather edge blade won't bleed as much as a wound caused by a slickly sharp broadhead. A slickly sharp broadhead makes deeper, cleaner cuts *and sends a minimum number of alarm bells* to the circulatory and nervous systems of the animal. This occurs no matter where in the body the animal is hit.

If the arrow remains in the ham as the animal moves, more cutting will occur, of course. This will also cause faster clotting. So if the broadhead is dull or has a feathered edge, you might be better off following that hit immediately, but waiting on a similar hit with a slickly sharp broadhead.

(A slickly sharp edge makes a cut which will heal faster than a rougher cut on non-fatal hits because there is less tissue damage, and the free-flowing blood washes the wound before finally clotting up. Compare a razorblade cut on your face to a scrape on your arm made by a blunt instrument and you will see a perfect example of this.)

After waiting the preferred time, stay cool. The urge is to take off like a pack of hounds, but that can be ruinous.

Take with you a small roll of toilet tissue for trail marking. (It is biodegradable, so it is not as critical that you go back over the trail and retrieve every tissue marker.) With plenty of trail markers, you can look back and easily determine whether the animal is curving in one direction or another. This is difficult to determine if you take only a couple of markers and leapfrog with them. You don't want to do much guessing on a blood trail, but if you lose it and have to guess, sometimes the long line of trail markers can help that guess.

If you plan to trail at night, use a gas lantern with half of the glass globe baffled so the light is projected ahead instead of in all directions. You can hold this light in front of you and see much better. The phosphorus in blood, especially fresh blood, shows up well at night. Flashlights are more difficult to work with because they generally don't throw as strong or as wide a beam of light, and some have a dark spot in the center of the beam.

A few people work better than a gang on a blood trail. Too many cooks spoil the broth, and too many trackers spoil the trail. The excitement is contagious and easily pushes things out of control, messing up the trail and possibly spooking the animal.

Begin at the site of the hit with what you already know. Mark, if possible, the last place you saw the animal, but don't assume that you've got the spot pinpointed. Look for blood or more hair (when cut, it doesn't always all fall to the ground at once) on the trail. Look on leaves, grass, bushes, saplings, tree trunks, rocks, sand, gravel, weeds, moss...everywhere. Be sure to check the undersides of leaves which have been kicked over by the animal's feet. Look

Look for blood on the undersides and tops of leaves that might have brushed against the animal's body as it moved past. Depending on where the animal was hit, sign may be higher or lower on vegetation along the trail.

to the sides of the trail, remembering the animal's body width and that the blood may spray to the side(s), fall straight down, or dribble down the animal's leg. Was the animal bleeding on left, right or both sides? If you don't know, you will have to check the trail. If the animal whirled after it was hit, you will want to check in a circle, for the blood may have sprayed.

Blood usually will be found on the side of the plant that the animal brushes against first, but not always. If the animal was hit high on the back or shoulder, look for blood at the appropriate height. There may not have been enough blood loss for blood to spill to the ground.

If there is a high back hit, you may need to check overhanging branches or brush. We trailed a bear once by trotting along and checking for blood at eye level—because the arrow made no bottom exit and the bear pumped blood out the top like a bellows as it ran.

The tracking crew must work together, not going too far ahead or apart from each other and making sure not to destroy any sign that they find.

A leg wound may cause the animal to favor that side, with the animal thus moving in an arc toward the wounded side.

No matter where the trail is, be sure to stay off it so sign is not destroyed. In fact, stay as far to the side of the trail as you feel you need to be to avoid destroying sign on or near the trail.If more than one person is working the trail, I feel most comfortable with a designated boss, probably keeping tight to the trail and making sure others are far enough to the side or behind so no sign is accidentally destroyed. No one should ever move ahead of the last sign found on the trail without being extraordinarily careful of where and how they move.

If you're trailing through fallen leaves, be careful to pick up your feet carefully and set them back down just as carefully. Shuffling through leaves can destroy or conceal a lot of sign accidentally.

If no blood or hair can be found, you have no choice but to search for tracks. A running animal may kick dirt, leaves or other material back as it takes off, but as it runs the force of the landing usually kicks material ahead or to the side, and any material on foot or hoof as the animal lifts it is pushed ahead of the track. This is helpful in determining direction of movement if the track is too faint.

Fresh soil or sand or other ground material kicked up should be darker than surrounding material, because it most likely will be more moist. This can help your trailing effort.

A running hoofed animal will spread its toes farther than will a walking animal, which may help in sorting out the right track where there are many tracks. Also, a wounded hoofed animal that is walking may spread its toes wide to help maintain its balance as it grows weaker.

In wet country, water dribbling back into an indistinguishable depression may be a clue to a fresh track. More than once, while trailing an animal through a swamp, the only sign I found was reeds pushed aside, water splashed here and there, and now and then a drop of blood floating on water. But that was enough sign.

If you cannot distinguish a track with your eyes, no matter what the soil or ground cover, stick your fingers into the suspected track. You might be able to feel toe prints or hoof prints.

Sometimes you read that wounded animals like to head for water. I'm not sure about that. The pronghorns I've shot tried to get away from the water just as fast as they could. Yeah, I know this is gross oversimplification, but I wanted to make a point. A wounded internal system may cause a rise in body temperature, so cooling water may be part of the defense mechanism. I'm more inclined to believe, though, that since water generally grows heavier vegetation the animal would be more likely to be heading for that cover than to the water.

Also, a wounded animal doesn't always run downhill or remain at the same elevation it was hit. Some animals spook in the direction their nose pointed when they were hit; others try to get back onto a trail, such as the trail they arrived on, most likely because they feel safe going back toward an area they just passed safely through. This spooked flight direction has done the most to create the "charge" of the wounded animal. I've seen mortally wounded animals head uphill for a saddle in a ridge, and if an animal feels safest in high ground...

Wounded animals will backtrack now and then, and I'm not speaking just of bears which will circle or backtrack and lay in wait for their tormentor. Circling probably is most common, principally as an attempt to get back to heavy cover. A deer hunting partner and I once tracked a deer in three circles inside a five-acre oak brush patch until we came to our senses. Don't ask me why both of us stayed on the trail and no one stayed behind to finish off the deer, especially after the first time we crossed our own tracks.

The main things are to take it slowly, mark the signs as needed, keep "helpers" from running ahead, be thorough and check everything. Then check again. Don't try to anticipate, and don't try to guess. Stick with the signs.

If you come to the end of a good trail and there suddenly is absolutely nothing, check one long leap to either side of the trail. I've found more than one deer which, as its last effort, made one big leap and crashed in or behind a brush pile or low spot farther to the side of the trail than would ordinarily be expected.

If you lose the trail, go back to the last known sign and either walk in increasing circles around that point or grid the area and methodically walk it. This is where help can make the job quicker.

We talked earlier of listening as well as looking. An animal hit from above, with no bottom exit hole, can go a long way without spilling blood. The last place you heard it move may be your best point to begin. You may also find the animal close by.

Four other aspects to be noted: 1) Weather, 2) other predators 3) scavengers, 3) late-afternoon hunts.

With approaching rain or snow, you don't have much choice about a lengthy wait before you begin trailing. All you can do is

Tracking snow (about one-to-three inches in depth) always puts a smile on a bowhunter's face. Not only does it make seeing a deer better, but it makes trailing an animal a lot easier.

get on the trail and be as cautious as possible to keep from spooking the animal into wild flight.

If you feel that coyotes or other predators have too good a chance to take your trophy, you may want to begin trailing earlier than recommended. This is a minor concern or no concern for most of our hunting efforts, but in some places it isn't.

Scavengers? Yes, crows and magpies can sometimes be used to locate a wounded or dead animal. I wonder, however, just how much I would want that animal if the scavengers had already found it. If, for instance, the animal was gut shot and is still alive, that's one thing, but if a couple of days have passed, the odds are for something much poorer. It's something to keep in mind, though.

Unless you know exactly where you are, and it is daylight, check your compass and landmarks frequently. You probably will be making many twists and turns as you follow the trail, paying close attention to the trail and none to where you are or are going. This can be troublesome in unfamiliar territory day or night, and troublesome at night in familiar territory.

Friend of mine and I got turned around one time following a blood trail less than 200 yards from my cabin. We followed the trail over a couple of small ridges and found the deer, but when it came time to drag out the deer after field dressing, we weren't sure which direction to go until we checked the stars. Naturally, since we were on completely familiar turf, we hadn't bothered to bring a compass.

Patience. Persistence. Thoroughness. We owe it to the game animal, to ourselves and to the sport of hunting to do the best we can every time.

15

Equipment Care Simplified

Taking care of your archery and bowhunting equipment is easy, especially if you keep an eye on things and practice preventive maintenance.

Remember that the equipment produced is almost always reliable, but nothing can be perfect. The only reason we're noting the obvious is because the remainder of this chapter will speak of problem avoidance, troubleshooting, etc. The concentration will be on problems and avoiding them, and that can make everything seem negative if not kept in perspective.

Bows

Know what the warranty covers and doesn't cover, and its length should anything major happen that might need repairing or replacing at the factory. Each bow has a stated draw weight, or minimum/maximum draw weight on adjustable bows. Don't abuse a compound's maximum weight, for that could over-stress the limbs or other items and cause breakage. If a bow is set above its recommended draw weight, you will most likely have voided the warranty.

Metal handles can break; wood handles can break. Limbs can delaminate or be cracked or bent before being taken from the box. As more and more are being made of fiberglass only, delamination ought to become less of a problem, but it will continue to exist. If

Lubricate moving parts on compond bows periodically to prevent wear and eliminate any noise.

something major such as this happens, check back with your dealer.

Keep bows with laminated parts (limbs and/or handle) away from heat. Don't lean them next to a camp fire. Don't store them in the back window of a vehicle, and be careful about storage in the trunk. In extremely hot weather, even storage in a trunk could cause problems.

Try not to leave recurve bows strung over long periods of time. Limbs can take a set which will reduce the bow's ability to store energy. This isn't anywhere near the concern it was years ago when manufacturing techniques weren't as refined, but it is still worth heeding. Longbows with little or no fiberglass are the most likely to take a set.

If a compound bow is to be stored, unused, for a long time, it is good sense to relax the limbs. Any reduction in limb stress ought to be good for long or short periods of time.

Don't overdraw compounds. The stress could make limbs or hardware come apart.

Keep an eye on compound cables for fraying. This isn't a big problem, but it happens. A weakened cable is a dangerous cable.

Lubricate the moving parts of compounds to reduce wear, rust and unwanted noise. Efficiency is also helped. Use oil for metal-to-metal wear, and powder or graphite for plastic-to-plastic or plastic-to-metal joints. There are lubricants on the market which have small Teflon beads in a fluid; this type of product is excellent.

When stringing any bow, be sure the limbs are not twisted during stringing, and keep your head safely away so any accident

Wax your bowstring frequently and check for frayed or cut strands. Don't let it get too worn before replacing it with a new one.

won't put your eyes out.

Hang bows in dry, cool places, from a peg hooked through the string or cable, or place them on two pegs positioned so the ends of the handles or bases of limbs rest on the pegs. Don't rest bows on a limb tip.

Keep Your Bowstring Waxed

Wax the string frequently and check for frayed or cut strands. A weakened bowstring is dangerous.

Be sure servings (the nylon or monofilament wound around end loops and middle where the arrow is nocked) are firm but not too tight. A too-tight serving pinches the strands and weakens them. Monofilament can work loose fairly easily; prevent this with a spot of glue if the serving looks like it needs it. If a serving is worn, replace it.

Clamp nock sets on the string snugly, but don't clamp them so tightly they pinch and weaken the strands.

Recurve bows apply friction on string loops and loop servings more than compounds because the string moves against the limb tip and strikes against the limb as the limbs recover. Check the loops for wear.

Check Your Accessories

Bow quivers, bow sights, cable guards, etc., can all work loose and rattle or not function properly. Check all screws for tightness before every use. A bit of Lok-Tite applied to each screw will hold them firmly in place, but not too firmly to back them out if you want to change something later.

Some of the metal used in bushings and bow handles is fairly soft, so when seating screws, don't bear down too much or you will strip the threads.

Bowsights range from inexpensively simple to highly adjustable and costly. Attach a pin guard, if you wish, to make sure pins aren't snagged and bent or broken accidentally. Soft, thin bow cases don't offer much protection; in fact, sight pins have ways of working right through the fabric like grasping little fingers. The best protection is to remove the sight and protect it with padding, or use a sturdy enough and large enough case to protect bow and sight together.

White appliance touch-up paint works well to highlight the sight pins when the original paint wears or chips off.

Be sure to check the batteries frequently if you are using lighted sights. Some lighted sight pins have wires which seem to tear loose always at the wrong time. (Make sure the state/province you are hunting in allows lighted sight pins. These pins are helpful in improving concentration and in seeing the pin under low-light conditions, but some agencies feel that the use of lighted sights means you're hunting after hours. However, using lighted sightpins doesn't improve your view of the game animal.)

Check the foam in the hood of your quiver and the clips which hold the shafts. Foam can get chopped up from repeated broadhead insertion and removal, which means it won't hold the broadheads as snugly and well protected as they should be. The rubber in the arrow clips can fatigue or become too stiff in cold weather. Neither condition is desirable.

Be sure, from the beginning, to have a quiver hood large enough to cover the entire broadhead blade.

Mount the quiver so it balances best and keeps nocks from striking the ground when the bow's lower limb tip is resting on the ground. Dirt fills these nocks, and the fletches can be dinged from the haphazard movement. If necessary, mount a bow quiver upside down, so nocks are up, to keep the nocks clean. This makes a nice debris-catching cup of the quiver hood, so it isn't the most desireable mounting position.

If you need or want to change an arrow rest, clean the sight window with rubbing alcohol. This will remove all adhesive residue from the previous arrow rest mounting and gives much better adhesion for the new rest.

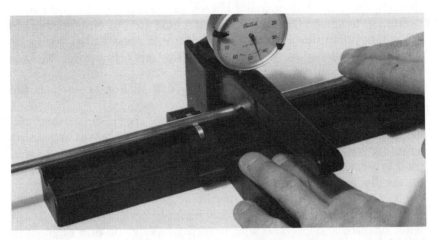

Check your arrows to make sure that they are not bent or warped. A straightening tool for aluminum arrows will more than pay for itself in time.

Arrows Need Care Too!

Aluminum arrows bend. They can all crack. Wood arrows can warp. Basically, though, all arrows are rugged and will last a long time if handled and used properly. But no arrow can be expected to be as good as new after colliding with a rock, a target support, etc. Sometimes a shaft bends or cracks when glanced off a tree trunk or stone.

To check for straightness, first sight down the shaft. If you are uncertain, roll the shaft across a flat surface without fletching or tip interference; or spin the shaft on your thumbnail; or hold the shaft against your palm or fingernail and blow on the fletching. If the arrow is bent it will rattle against the V of your nails.

Aluminum shafts of certain types and hardnesses of alloy are much easier to straighten than the softer alloys. Straightening tools are available for home use. Wood shafts can sometimes be straightened by steaming and bending, much as the Indians steamed and bent wood strips for canoe ribs.

Nocks are soft plastic and can be cut, bent or broken when struck. Check them often. They can be easily replaced. Spare nocks and a tube of glue are handy things to have in your field pack.

Fletching can rip or be cut, especially during broadhead practice sessions when groups are looking nice.

Damaged plastic fletching ought to be replaced, but if the

fletches are wrinkled or matted, they can usually be brought back to life, so to speak. To do this, bring a tea kettle of water to boil so the steam pours out the spout. Rotate the feathers in the steam, at whichever distance works best, until the feathers spring back to good shape.

Don't shoot cracked arrows. They can shatter as soon as the bowstring is released.

Dirty arrows, marked with dirt or blood, should be washed and cleaned. During practice sessions, especially when you are stump shooting or shooting at targets on the ground, carry an old toothbrush to clean dirt from the shaft, fletching and point. This is especially useful when cleaning out broadheads used in practice, for they can clog with plenty of dirt.

Sharp broadheads carried for hunting should oiled and left bare, or oiled and covered with masking tape if you don't expect to use them for awhile. Just remember to remove the tape before attempting to shoot any game animal. That little detail has been overlooked by more than one bowhunter, and none of them were very happy with the results. Don't cover the edges with Vaseline or other grease, because that material will pick up dirt and chaff by the bucketful, or so it seems.

Carry a small pliers with you to help remove points from stumps, saplings, etc. You might also want a T-shaped item which screws onto the threaded ferrule after the arrow is screwed off. Made of steel, the devise gives much more leverage and power than the arrow shaft would permit.

Every broadhead shot should be inspected for continued straightness afterward. Bent broadheads sometimes become small game heads, but most end up in the garbage.

Transport and store your arrows in a cardboard box or plastic tube. The container isn't important, except it must be sturdy enough to meet whatever transportation needs you have at the moment. No matter what the arrows are protected by, they *must* have some sort of slotted dividers to hold them securely yet keep them from touching each other.

Leather tabs can become too creased to allow a smooth, crisp release. If a leather tab becomes soaked, such as when you're hunting or practicing in the rain, dry it like any leather and recondition it. Or use a soft plastic tab and eliminate the worry. (This tab is especially nice when you are bowfishing, because the constant wetness softens your hands, which then require more protection from the bowstring.)

16

Safety First & Last

One aspect of bowhunting that is rarely discussed by bowhunters is hunting accidents.

It makes sense really, because accidents always happen to someone else. Right?

Wrong! And that's why I'm covering them here; to remind you that hunting accidents can happen to you and make you aware of things you can do to prevent them from permanently changing or even ending your life. You know the old saying "An ounce of prevention is worth more than a pound of cure."

Don't underestimate that statement, it could have saved Gary Howard's life.

Gary, a 35-year-old husband and father, was killed near Fort Wayne, Indiana during the 1986 bow season. Gary wasn't doing anything wrong, he was just sneaking to his stand along a familiar trail, looking forward to spending another fall day afield.

What happened? Another hunter mistook Gary's fully camouflaged form for that of a deer's and drove an arrow through his heart. Apparently, the fact that legal shooting time had not arrived didn't bother the man.

What could have Gary done? I don't know for sure, but I suspect the shooting would not have occurred if he was carrying a small flashlight. He may not have needed it to find his way around the dark woods, and it may have spooked a deer or two, but it could have prevented his death. I suggest you bring one, it might save your life someday.

Bowhunting safety, for the most part, is common sense and knowledge of your equipment. Sure, accidents can happen, but you can greatly lessen your chances of being involved in one if you know what to be on the watch for.

Equipment Checklist

1) Watch for cracks that can develop in the limbs or handle of your bow. Most hairline cracks aren't dangerous, but if you are uncertain take the bow to your dealer and ask him.

2) Never "shoot" a bow without an arrow on the string, the bow could literally explode in your hand. Never over-draw a short bow, it could lead to bow breakage.

3) Always use a bowstringer when stringing a recurve or longbow. It's easier, more secure and won't twist limbs. Check both tips of the bow to make sure the string is properly positioned.

4) Use the recommended string length for your bow. A bowstring that is too short may lead to over-drawing your bow. A bowstring that is too long will slap your hand when you shoot.

Hunting Situations

1) Always carry your broadheads in a quiver with a hood that protects your broadheads and yourself in case of a fall. Be extra cautious when handling broadheads. Some of the models which use inserted razorblades are difficult to assemble. Take it slow and easy, and always use a broadhead wrench when tightening them onto the arrow.

2) Never run, cross a fence or stream, or enter camp with an arrow nocked. A bow with a nocked arrow is as potentially dangerous as a loaded firearm; treat it with the same respect.

3) Don't shoot arrows straight up; they tend to come down the same way. When shooting at squirrels, raccoons or other game in tree tops, make sure of your background. Some of the hunting bows used today can shoot an arrow over 200 yards!

4) Be careful when hunting in areas with heavy hunting pressure. If you are wearing the proper camouflage and moving slowly, you will be hard to see and look like a deer. Be especially careful in low light situations. I recommend you carry a small flashlight when moving to and from your stand.

5) Always be sure of your target. Never shoot at a sound or movement in the brush. If you're in a bull- or buck-only zone,

Push-pins painted with a reflective coating work well in marking the trail to your stand. They are less noticeable by other bowhunters and when entering or leaving in low light will show up extremely well in a flashlight beam.

make sure the animal has antlers. If you're bear hunting, make sure you don't shoot a cub or a sow with cubs. Above all, if something doesn't feel right, *don't shoot!*

Treestand Safety

1) Use a rope to lift bow, arrows and other gear up to your treestand. Never climb into an elevated stand with equipment in your hand. The same goes for descending. Be extra careful when the bark is slick because of rain or snow.

2) Use a safety strap to tie yourself to the tree in case you fall asleep or your stand gives way. *This is very important.*

According to the Shepard Spinal Center in Atlanta, Georgia, the nation's largest center for patients paralyzed by spinal cord injury, accident percentages involving treestands has grown tremendously in recent years.

In Georgia, for example, 29-percent of the total deer hunting accidents during the 1981-82 hunting season involved treestands. In 1986, 42-percent of the deer hunting accidents involved treestands.

Carpeting firmly attached to your portable treestand platform will give you better footing and eliminate any noise you may make if you change your position. If hunting in snow country, make sure the platform doesn't get compacted with snow or ice.

Although most injuries from a treestand accident are relatively minor, the number of people sustaining permanent paralysis from spinal cord injury is increasing.

Falls from treestands account for over 44-percent of the total number of treestand accidents, with one out of every five falls resulting in permanent paralysis.

Most of these falls occur when the hunter is tired and puts his foot where there isn't any stand, or simply shifts his weight and falls. Some hunters have actually fallen asleep, only to wake up on the ground 10 or 15 feet below. Some fall even further.

David Renz, of Dalton, Georgia, was hunting from a stand in a tall hickory when he took his plunge.

"The stand I was on was the tallest I'd ever built—29 feet high. I dozed off, rolled completely sideways and never woke up until I hit the ground. I hit one limb about 10 feet from the bottom of the tree. I put a gash in my head that I could lay three fingers in. It required 28 stitches to close."

David also crushed three vertebrae in his back, broke seven

ribs and his arm. A collapsed lung kept him in intensive care for awhile. He is now a paraplegic and confined to a wheelchair.

Safety When The Animal Is Down

1) Always approach a downed animal cautiously. Even a "dead" animal can nail you with its hooves or antlers. Bill Ruzicka, a Minnesota bowhunter, found that out a few years ago when he straddled a head-shot whitetail buck to field dress it.

"He was twitching a little bit," Bill explained, "but I figured he was down for the count. It just blew my mind when his rear hoof came up and ripped the glasses off my face. He looked like a rabbit trying to scratch his ear. A couple inches over and he would have killed me."

The best way to approach a downed animal is from the back side, with its legs away from you. If you're not sure the animal is dead, touch its eye with a long stick. If the animal blinks, it is still alive. Don't hesitate to shoot again.

2) Before gutting your animal, determine if your broadhead is still inside the animal. You could save yourself a nasty gash or even the loss of a couple of fingers. NAHC Associate Editor Steve Pennaz recalls the only time he forgot to look.

"A few years ago, I shot a big doe just before dark. I didn't have a flashlight, so I headed back to the cabin to find one. My brother was there and so was a friend; naturally they came to help.

"The doe was standing in a field of tall grass when I shot, so it was difficult to find the blood trail, which really surprised me because I saw the arrow sticking out of her chest when she ran. I was just starting to second guess my hit when my brother found my arrow shaft—or what was left of it. The broadhead and about seven inches of the shaft were missing.

"We found the deer about 20 minutes later, and in the excitement forgot about the missing section of the arrow shaft. I was reminded of it a few minutes later when I was gutting her.

"Everything was out except the heart and lungs, so I reached to pull them out. That's when I grabbed the broadhead.

"I was shooting the Savora Super S back then, which has razorblade inserts. I didn't cut myself too badly, because the head broke bone on the way in and was pretty busted up. But talk about getting scared. I could have lost a finger, or worse."

Basic Woodsmanship

1) Carry a map of the area you are hunting, a compass (and

When there are others in your hunting party it is always wise to have a good idea of where everyone will be and have a designated meeting place when you're through hunting for the day.

know how to use it), matches and other survival gear. Should you get lost, don't panic. Sit down and think about your options. If night is falling, build a shelter and gather enough firewood to last until morning.

2) If you are hunting alone, let others know where you are hunting and when you will return. A lot of weird things can happen during a bowhunting trip. Wisconsin bowhunter Chad Owens can testify to that.

Chad was hunting deer in some woods that surrounds his parent's farm near Cumberland, when a bolt of lightning blew him out of his treestand. Dazed and in pain, the 16-year-old hunter wandered away.

Jon Owens, Chad's father, went to look for his son when Chad failed to return home after dark. Luckily, he found Chad a half hour later.

Chad spent the next five days in the hospital—two of them in intensive care. But he was lucky; lucky that his father knew where he was and how to find him.

17

Gaining
The Landowner's Blessing

W hy, you may be thinking, have we devoted an entire chapter
on gaining landowner permission to hunt?

Several reasons.

First, nobody's making any more land, but lots of people are
putting up more "No Hunting" signs. Sometimes those signs go
up because of too much hunting pressure; sometimes because of
poor hunter behavior on the land in previous seasons and
sometimes because the landowner feels that since he owns it
everybody else ought to stay off.

Second, increasing hunter numbers create additional hunting
pressure on the available hunting land — private *and* public.
Landowners who *do* give permission to hunters are going to reach
a point where they logically say "That's enough. My land can't
take any more hunters without ruining it for all of them."

It seems reasonable to believe that the hunter who best knows
the landowners and is trusted by them is the hunter who will have
the best chance of continuing to gain permission to hunt on private
land.

Not a lot of areas feel this intensity of pressure during
bowhunting, but some do and more will in the future. Many
bowhunters got into this sport simply because they were tired of
the incredible hunting pressure during firearms season. We're
speaking mainly of deer season, of course, but that's the *number*

one big game animal, so we're talking also of the prime opportunity for hunting pressure to develop.

Third, leasing hunting land will become more common each year. In some areas, such as Texas, right now this practice is about the only way you're going to be able to hunt on private land. Leasing will become more common in areas where there is little public land to hunt. As more landowners realize that the wild game their land supports can be a cash crop, we will see more and more lease programs. This, at the very least, gives a landowner an opportunity to offset whatever crop damage losses he may encounter from high game populations.

Fourth, access to some public land — particularly in the West — is controlled, right or wrong, by people with grazing leases. Access over this land can get to be a sticky problem. We certainly can't solve it here, but as outdoor recreationists (hunters and other sports participants) we need to be aware of and concerned about it. That's *our* land we're sometimes being kept from.

Fifth, private land — large and small tracts — can have excellent hunting, especially in suburban areas or on suburban fringes where pockets of prime habitat often exist, where firearms often are not allowed and where the hunting pressure is sometimes light. (Probably heavy on evenings and weekends, but light on weekday mornings.)

Finally, without land to hunt on there is no hunting, no matter how much you have practiced your shooting. Public lands cannot support all the hunting pressure in most areas. Yes, I know that some states, such as Nevada, are mainly public land — but this is small comfort to a Georgia or Connecticut bowhunter. Without land to hunt on, there is no hunting. Period. That's a scary thought.

Need any more reasons?

So what can you do of a positive nature?

Respect the landowner, his property and his rights, for openers. I've been on both sides of the fence, so I believe I can see the concerns from both sides. I grew up on a dairy and hog farm that fortunately had about 70 acres of swamp, wooded ridges, a trout creek, tag alders and brush. Because of that terrain, I could hunt grouse, rabbits, squirrels, pheasants and deer right on the farm. So could a lot of other people, but few stopped to ask. They usually parked just over the ridge about half a mile from the buildings and out of sight. So you know they felt guilty about not asking for permission.

Hayfields aren't parking lots, nor are they large, open

turn-around areas for vehicles. Neither are oats or wheat fields. They're money. They are livestock feed. But you would not have known that by some of the destruction we had from time to time. Nor are ripe ears of corn grown for dog-less pheasant hunters to hurl through standing corn in hopes of flushing pheasants.

Griping? Yes and no. Not everyone did that, but enough did. One rotten apple....you know.

When you're not the landowner, the thought often is "Gee, we're not going to hurt anything. So is it that big a deal?"

You might know you're not going to hurt anything, but does the landowner know it? As litigation-crazy as this society is today, if a landowner is going to err he's going to err on the side of caution. It is, after all, *his* property.

Ask permission! You won't be allowed to hunt every place you ask — but remember, not even Ty Cobb batted 1,000. If you get turned down, accept it and continue looking.

When you have permission, it frees your mind to concentrate on scouting and hunting. It just can't be that much fun hunting with a cloud of "scram if we're seen" concern hanging overhead. With permission, you will do a better job, enjoy it more, and possibly be more successful. You also will be doing all hunters, not just yourself, a big favor.

Get that permission early. One day before the season opens isn't early. It leaves a negative feeling with you and with the landowner, who probably already has given permission to others who did ask early. Yes, I know hunters have gone out west, asked a rancher for permission to hunt and been granted it, but that's more an exception than a rule.

For deer hunting, as an example, you might want to start right with your late season scouting. Maybe you've already looked at topographical maps and aerial photos, so you have an idea of what to expect. Tell the landowner your purpose, let him know that you have done a little homework, and tell him that if his land looks interesting you would like to be able to hunt it next fall. It seems reasonable to believe that anyone doing this much preparation is serious about his sport and an above-average bet that he will be a decent person to grant trespass permission.

Find out whether the landowner allows only doe shooting, only buck shooting, or both. You could earn a fast exit if you unknowingly violate the landowner's rule.

Some hunters I know buy extra aerial photos of the land they want to get permission to scout and then, if it looks promising,

Obtaining permission to hunt on a landowner's property is not only common courtesy, in many states it is the law. It's your choice if you want to pass up a good looking spot to hunt on if you don't want to bother to ask permission. On the other hand, you'll never know if you don't ask.

permission to hunt. They give one of the extra photos to the landowner, who probably had never gotten around to getting such a photo for himself.

Tell the landowner you will let him know in advance each time you go on his land. This may be difficult, impractical or impossible with absentee landowners, but if the owner lives right there, by all means do so. Let him know where you plan to be. If he has any objections, you can find a solution then with a much calmer air.

Park the vehicle near the landowner's buildings if you can. He will feel better, and your scouting/hunting efforts won't be as visible to other hunters.

Give the landowner your business card if you have one. Give him a paper with your name, address and phone number written on it, plus the make, model and description of your vehicle, and the license number.

Find out whether the landowner minds your arriving at early hours and leaving late. If I were a landowner and my dog barked at 5 a.m. but I wasn't expecting it, I would be a bit concerned.

When you must open gates, close them immediately after you have driven through — unless you enjoy dealing with angry livestock owners whom you must help round up loose cattle.

On your scouting and hunting trips, keep an eye out for anything out of the ordinary regarding the landowner's fences, cattle in the back pasture, or whatever. Much as he wants to, he cannot keep an eye on everything all the time, and he will appreciate the information.

Dress decently and act the same. You don't need to be wearing hunting clothes to ask permission, nor do you need to be dressed up. All you want to be is a regular guy, so be one.

Remember, too, that if you are granted permission, *you*—not you and all your friends—have permission.

You will want to know something about the landowner and—if he is a farmer or rancher—stock, crops, markets and such, but don't attempt to come on like an expert unless you are, and even then it would be a good idea to feel your way along. Making a fool of yourself isn't supposed to be part of the program.

If you offer to help with farm or ranch work, be sure you will be a help instead of a hindrance.

Getting to know landowners is just plain common sense. Easy conversation among comfortable acquaintances is nice. (Even when you arrive to scout or hunt but find the landowner wants to shoot the breeze a while, give up some of your time when it is the sensible thing to do.)

What about gifts? Well, you cannot buy friendship or respect, but you can give useful items which show your appreciation. A smoked turkey sits well on anyone's table, for instance. If you want to give the landowner some meat from an animal you have taken from his land, ask him first if he wants it. Liquor or beer usually is a no-no, but people have been known to share a beer or soft drink when they are standing around the truck talking after the scouting run or hunt.

Build a solid, trusting relationship. You never know when one landowner might suggest you ask a neighbor about that neighbor's land. That can be an unanticipated benefit.

You consider yourself "just folks." That's all landowners are, too. But they do hold the key that you are politely asking them to turn and unlock their land.

18

Techniques For
Bowhunting Small Game

In the overall scheme of bowhunting, small game and similar species are usually shoved down the ladder a ways. It's tough for a woodchuck, ground squirrel, gray squirrel, prairie dog, grouse or gopher to compete with the bugle of a bull elk or the whack of whitetail antlers.

However....and this is a big however....there is more here than we tend to think of, for the same reason a five dollar bill is more impressive than 500 pennies. Add up all the bits and pieces of great times and great learning sessions gleaned from small game and other species hunted in our bowhunting careers and the lessons and memories are mighty.

I firmly believe that if many of today's bowhunters spent less time searching for and dreaming only about that trophy whitetail, muley, elk or whatever big game species they prefer, and spent more time with small game and other general bowhunting opportunities, they would become better all-around bowhunters, and because of that ultimately have a better chance at a trophy animal whey they do hunt for it.

Whether you get your small game as a bonus while big game hunting, or specifically go after small game, the emphasis is on sport and the hunt. It has to be, for there sure isn't much meat for the pot involved when we go after small game with bow and arrow. You can, though, learn quite a bit about spotting game, stalking, positioning yourself for good shots, scouting, feeding patterns and other behavioral patterns, the value of patience and planning and attention to details required for consistently successful bowhunting.

Toss in the hunting skills learned by going after non-game species such as woodchucks (young ones are good eating, too, if cared for properly), ground squirrels, gophers and such. How about the shooting practice you will get with prairie dogs? (Please explain to me why I can miss a pronghorn buck at 25 yards one day and plunk a prairie dog at 30 yards the next.)

A friend suggests that if you want to help a kid learn to be a good hunter, give him/her a camera with a regular lens and tell that kid to bring you a close-up photo of a squirrel. Good point. Small game hunting with bow and arrow is just about the same....a lot of hours spent learning, spent having fun, spent getting frustrated.

What about varmint calling? Foxes, coyotes, raccoons, bobcats.

What about going after pheasants?

Armadillos, known years ago as "Hoover Hogs," offer target practice and some laid back hunting practice for Texas bowhunters now and then.

There obviously is no dearth of hunting opportunities and shooting practice. We're limited mainly by our resourcefulness and the time we have or want to devote to it.

Each part of the country has small game and "other" species which are not on any protected list and thus make eligible targets for kids and grown bowhunters. We cannot hope to talk about each of them here, but we hope to firmly establish the idea—if it isn't already firmly planted—that the bow does not need to be hung up or aimed only at paper or 3D targets after big game seasons close, or when you are deer hunting, for instance, only deer can be hunted or paid attention to.

For instance, on my first hunt for pronghorns, I discovered where most of North America's cottontail rabbits live—out west. Brush country boys who live further east like to talk about rabbits and rabbit hunting, and I knew something about rabbit hunting, but this was an eye opener. The first couple of times you encounter all those rabbits, you will find it difficult to believe that many rabbits could and would hide out in such an area and run so little.

Get permission to hunt, and then slowly search the alfalfa fields, hay stacks, ranch building perimeters and corrals. This makes a great break from big game hunting, and is almost a social activity.

Bowhunting for small game sharpens your hunting and shooting skills as well as provides good eating.

Later in the winter, when the cottontails and jackrabbits gather in some of the lowlands and flats, there are herds of hares and such. Kick a sage bush and it kicks back or runs away, more or less. If I could afford the time, I would take a week in mid-winter and travel a long way just to shoot rabbits in those settings.

Small Game Equipment

Is there such a setup as "small game bowhunting equipment?" Yeah; it's the same as your big game hunting equipment, maybe toned down a bit in draw weight if you're accustomed to Old Herniator weights for deer or elk or such. (Old Herniator is a cousin to Eye Bulger and Toe Crosser, draw weights in the 80-, 90- and 100-pound ranges.) On the other hand, if you like skipping arrows a long, long way or pulling them from deep in the earth, keep the weight where it was for big game and your muscles won't lose their tone.)

There is not much sense switching to a lighter draw weight and lighter arrows just because you will be hunting small game. You want to keep yourself totally comfortable with your hunting bow and how it shoots. You know the right sight pictures, the trajectory, the feel at full draw, and you want to maintain those muscle memories and subconscious controls.

One thing you will change—your arrows. This is the time for junker arrows, or at least much less expensive ones. You *will* lose arrows; an arrow can give lessons to rabbits about disappearing in grass. (Check a big game hunter's quiver sometime. If a couple of wood arrows are stashed there, you know he won't pass up a good small game shot.)

Some bowhunters like to use blunts for small game and other non-game hunting; others prefer field points; still others stick with broadheads. Whatever the tip, there often is enhancement, such as a metal washer behind a blunt, or wire prongs behind a field point, or a washer behind a broadhead (to inhibit penetration and provide more shock). Blunts may, for instance, break a leg or wing upon impact, or knock the animal for a loop, but not stop it so you can recover it. A field point simply may poke a hole in the animal and let it escape if it isn't pinned to the ground. A broadhead may zip on through, surely killing the animal but allowing it to run off and hide. The enhancements help solve those problems. A Judo Point also makes a good small game head because it packs a wallop and the wire prongs stop the arrow quickly, snagging on grass, leaves or brush.

Pre-formed metal pieces as shown here can be attached to your arrows for extra shocking power when hunting small game. They can be used behind any style head, even a broadhead.

If you are shooting at flying birds, you have set yourself a supreme challenge. Arrow tips with wire loops added to the blunt or other basic tip will increase the impact area and may help knock down a bird that otherwise would be missed or only nicked.

Most arrows used in small game hunting will be fletched regularly, but consider flu-flu arrows for flying birds or shots at targets in trees. Flu-flu's will make the arrows fall where they can be recovered. The flu-flus range is limited, of course, by the huge air drag created, and it is a noisy arrow. Consider the options and decide what is best for the situation.

Pheasant hunting with a gunning partner can offer good wing shooting and meat for the freezer. Dick Wilson, a Nevada-based bowhunting friend, hunts this way. The bowhunter always takes the first shot and the gunner second. Each gets plenty of action, because the bowhunter isn't going to bag many birds. A flushed pheasant often likes to launch straight up, then level out and fly off. This levelling-off point offers an instant when the bird is basically hanging in the air. The trick is to time your shot so the arrow arrives at that instant. If this bird take-off doesn't happen, then you have a regular shot at a flying bird.

Good practice targets for bird hunting are heavy, round chunks of cardboard tossed in the air. Round foam targets also are available, or you can carve your own.

Hunting for predators adds a rare twist to non-game hunting, for here the hunter becomes the hunted. Settle down into a camouflaged shooting position and squall like a hurt rabbit; the fox or coyote or bobcat may come in at a dead run or it may sneak

Bagging a few bushy tails can offer a change of pace from bowhunting big game.

in and you won't even see it.

This type of hunting may work best with a partner, one of you to do the calling and the other to position himself away from the caller and in good position for shooting. The incoming animal's attention will be focused on the call, so the shooter should get a better opportunity to draw, aim and release. If electronic callers are legal in your area, those devices will accomplish the same thing for a solo hunter.

Rabbits and squirrels are the small game targets most often hunted on purpose. Most of us cut our eyeteeth on them, with gun and/or bow, because they are the most widespread. Rabbits hunted in tandem with a gunning friend can offer good action and a better promise of meat for the freezer. Whether you post one person and the other checks out grass clumps, fence rows and brush piles, or whether you walk the area together, you should have action....fast action of the here-it-comes-there-it-goes variety. A slow-moving beagle might be just the ticket here, especially if you are hunting alone.

Whenever you are hunting in tandem with a gunner, be sure you know where each other is at all times and what the shooting rules are. This is only common sense and good safety precaution.

I never bothered with squirrels at all until one morning on a deer stand, when I realized that I had been watching grays for two solid hours. Naturally, no one wants to ruin a chance at a deer by flinging an arrow at a squirrel, but if you are as careful in moving to shoot at the squirrel as you would be at a deer, you should do just fine. Release the arrow and don't move; even if you miss the squirrel won't be more than a little startled.

A couple of years ago, while I was standing next to an oak tree waiting for deer to move past on a trail some 20 yards away, a gray squirrel hopped and scurried its way within range. When it had its head buried in leaves, looking for an acorn, I shot at it. The arrow buried in leaves right under the squirrel's belly. It leaped, spotted a fallen log with a hole in it, and dashed into that hole.

I kept that squirrel in the log for 10 minutes. Every time it worked up nerve to poke its nose out, I twitched my bow and the squirrel retreated.

Missed it again when it dashed out, too.

Best squirrel hunting is done sitting and watching in feeding areas such as nut groves or cornfield edges. A squirrel call can enhance things now and then, especially on young squirrels and early in the season before the bushy-tails have been popped at much.

Despite my best intentions, I know that most of the small game I take will be during big game season. A ruffed grouse walks below my treestand...a squirrel looks for acorns only 10 yards away. I can't resist, so I wait for the proper time and pop one. Same for grouse on mountain hunts, or ptarmigan on highest elevations or tundra.

The targets may be smaller, game or non-game, but the essential ingredients are all there—patience, perseverance, learn the intended quarry's habits and actions, and enjoy the challenge of the hunt. You will be frustrated beyond belief at times, but the shooting and learning opportunities ought to be numerous, and the paybacks immediate and on later hunts for bigger game.

19

Bowfishing Is
Available To Everyone

Bowfishing is a sleeper. Not every bowhunter around the country lives in a good bowfishing area, but most do. There is more good bowfishing available than many bowhunters realize. Just examine the widespread domain of the carp and you'll see, and that's just for openers.

Consider, too, that bowfishing often gives you more good hunting, shooting practice (as opposed to paper or 3D targets) in a half an hour than would be offered during a couple seasons of deer hunting. Small game hunting can provide many shots, but not come anywhere near matching the action of carp at spawning time. It's good shooting, too, because you get caught up in the excitement of actual moving targets that can get out of the way of your arrow. Of course, it's always fun to see who can get the biggest fish.

The action can be nearly year-round. Spring spawning runs produce the most bowfishing, understandably, but mid-summer and autumn hunting — which it is when fish aren't spawning — offers action. There can be winter action, even in the north where dam overflows or hot-water outlets or just plain fast water keep ice off. A few bowhunters have even been known to bore holes in the ice and watch for carp to swim past. This takes a special dedication. Or something.

Bowfishing can become a fever. I know half a dozen

A top bowfishing trophy is alligator gar, inhabiting the coastal waters and fresh-water rivers of the South.

bowhunters who would just as soon go after a hog carp as a trophy deer. They have to hunt for the hog carp, preferring to do it in the non-spawning times, and they like this particular challenge.

In freshwater there are carp, suckers, redhorse, stonerollers (a bottom-hugging sucker), several species of gar, turtles, game fish in a few states and provinces, frogs and dogfish. In saltwater, you will find shark, ocean sunfish, rays, and in a few spots in the Gulf of Mexico a fish called the tripletail.

I imagine I've left out a few species, too.

Bowfishing is just plain pure fun, as well as good off-season hunting/shooting practice. It can be sociable — few bowfishermen go out alone. It is relaxing, because most of the action occurs before mosquitoes get going. It generally occurs during good weather, at times when you feel good just being on the water. I remember watching the sun come up golden over Wisconsin's Green Bay one June morning. The only ripples on the water were made by spawning carp...the only ripples, that is, until we started after them. Then there was considerable splashing. We took about 400 pounds of carp by noon.

There can be adventure to bowfishing, too. I've bowfished for sharks off Florida and California but have yet to connect. We got close to a hammerhead off Pensacola, and we ran into a red tide off California. A red tide screws up everything.

I will not, however, forget chumming in a huge circle, almost but not quite closing the circle—so a shark picking up the chum line would be directed to come from only one direction, with us looking in that direction. We bobbed at the end of the chum line in a good big-water craft, but I still felt like the ultimate large chunk of chum, waiting at the end of the line for a toothy predator with staring eyes and replaceable teeth and absolutely no concern or remorse. We waited and watched. I listened to more-experienced guys tell of hooking sharks, pulling them to the boat, slashing open the shark's belly, cutting the line and jumping back...jumping back to watch the riveting scene of a shark driven to a feeding frenzy by the smell of blood—its own blood—and consuming its own entrails as they floated free of its ripped belly.

Such are the worlds of man and shark when they meet, predator and predator.

Bowfishing Tackle

Bowfishing tackle is specialized, but there is plenty of room for you to express your own opinion.

Bow. You can use either compound or recurve. I prefer a recurve because there are no cables and such for the bowfishing line to snag on, much of the shooting is snap shooting—which is easier with a recurve, and the recurves are easier to clean of water and debris than are compounds.

Some bowfishermen prefer short compounds in the 50-pound draw weight range, especially when they are bowfishing from a canoe or other easily moved craft. They can come to full draw and stand in the bow of the craft like a poised heron while their partner in the stern pushes them silently in among the fish. The fairly light draw weight is easy to hold for a long time, if needed, yet has the power to give good arrow penetration on fish a couple of feet below the water surface.

Reels. Bowfishing reels today are more sophisticated than before. There are shoot-through, shoot-over, shoot-under and shoot-beside models. Most have a threaded mounting bolt that screws into the stabilizer hole on your bow, or a side-mount plate

Shoot-through reel style bowfishing rig.

that can be attached to the holes for a bowsight mount. You won't find many tape-on reels today, but they are available.

These reel types require that you hand-wind the line onto the spool. They are all-metal units, wire-and-rubber cages or plastic molded models. Most have a metal clip or slit rubber finger to hold the line loosely so the loops of line don't fall from the reel.

Some bowfishermen mount big, closed-face spinning reels on a stubby bracket which screws into the stabilizer hole. These reels are filled with heavy monofilament line, rarely under 30-pound test. If you try this style reel, don't fill up the reel, and experiment with 30-, 40- or 50-pound mono (or heavier, if you wish), depending upon how you bowfish and the area in which you will be fishing. A heavy line will help yank the arrow free from brush and heavy grass, but heavier line won't pay out as easily when you shoot because it takes a set, and you cannot get as much of it onto a spool.

Best size and type of reel is personal preference. Manufacturers of the wire/rubber frame reels say the line dries better on their models, preventing rot. Others point out the amount of line their

Other bowfishing setups include (left to right) a large spin-cast reel, shoot-over and shoot-beside models.

reel can hold and its corresponding ability to pay off line with little drag.

If you are using a closed-face spinning reel, remember to push the release button before each shot. If you forget, you will forget only once. When you forget, the arrow comes flying back past you faster than it left.

Another safety tip: When using drum-type reels, be sure no line is looped around a finger or thumb when you release the bowstring. Those loops are painful; I speak from experience.

Rods. Bowfishing rods are used more and more. They are used with a closed-face reel, and they screw into the reel mount. They usually are 24 inches long, of tubular aluminum or fiberglass, with threaded insert base and a big rod-tip ferrule on the tip. The rod reduces the chance that line will loop around your reel and take some of the strain off the line when fighting a big fish.

Arrows. Fish arrows usually are solid fiberglass with a regular nock and slip-over rubber fletching. The fletching looks good, but I think the looks are more than the function. Shots generally are short and the line provides stabilizing drag. You might want to

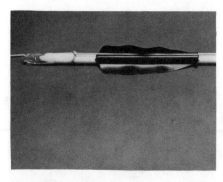

Bowfishing arrows are usually solid fiberglass with a regular nock and slip-over rubber fletching. Note that the line runs the full length of the arrow and is secured just ahead of the nock.

remove the fletching.

Points. Fish points almost always are conical, but there may be a flat, barbed style available. Some have one barb, some have two barbs; some have retractable barbs, some have fixed barbs. Whatever style you use, *keep the point sharp.* Fish scales are tough. (Ancient Indians used scales from the alligator gar as protection on breastplates they wore to war.)

Fortunately, almost all fish points have screw-off heads or retractable or reversible barbs. A solid·point with a fixed barb is tough, slow and messy removing from a fish. The threaded male part should be on the section of the point mounted on the shaft; the point screws onto it. With a reverse style, there's much more tendency for the threads to jam into the base unit and lock up.

The best finger protection is a plastic finger tab, impervious to water. This gives a smoother release than a creased, wet leather tab, and wet, bare fingers get too soft to shoot comfortably for long.

Rigging Your Fish Arrow

Glue the head to the shaft when the head is one piece. On a two-piece, screw-together head, glue the base to the shaft, then drill the hole through base and shaft. No matter what the setup, always have the hole through head and shaft. This insures that the fish will stay on the line should the head slip off the arrow shaft or the shaft break.

You can simply run the line through the hole in the back of the shaft and then down through the hole at the tip, then tie it off. A sliding setup is better, though, in keeping line away from your fingers and away from the reel. Get some seven-strand wire, a few metal pinch clamps, some double-loop (non-snap) fishing swivels

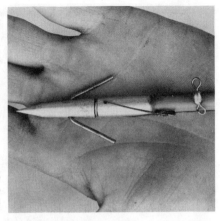

A good bowfishing head will unscrew so the barbs can be reversed, making removal of the arrow from the fish much easier.

and several pop-top rings from beer or soft-drink cans.

Run one end of the wire through a clamp, through the hole in the arrow near the point and back in the metal clamp. Pinch the clamp tight with a pliers, pinching parallel between the wires so it tightens on both.

Remove the rubber fletching, slip on a pop-top ring (with tab twisted off). Cut the wire about six inches *shorter* than the arrow. Slip on another clamp, run the wire through the ring, through the swivel and back into the clamp. Pinch it tight and you are rigged. Tie your fish line to the other end of the double swivel and the job is done.

This rig allows the line to stay on the reel until you shoot. The ring slides down the arrow as you draw and keeps the line out in front of your hand instead of dangling between drawing hand and the reel.

Another style is to use stainless steel leader wire, clamped with the metal clamps after it is run through holes fore and aft on the fish arrow. The leader wire runs fairly taut along the shaft. A double-loop (non-snap) swivel has the steel leader threaded through one loop; your fishing line is tied to the other loop. The swivel slides down the leader as you draw.

Where To Aim

The key to hitting fish with an arrow is to aim lower than you think you should. Light refraction in water—which makes the fish appear closer to the surface than it actually is—will fool you. The deeper the fish or the longer the shot, the farther below it you must aim.

A canoe with a foam-supported shooting platform is an excellent bowfishing craft. Note the extra long paddle for maneuvering the canoe while standing up; and a tub for the fish.

Rule of thumb is to aim four inches low (below the image of the fish) for every foot of water depth on a 10-foot shot. For a 20-foot shot, aim eight inches low for each foot of water depth; on a five-foot shot, aim two inches low for each foot of water depth. Adjusting from the basic 10/4 rule is just multiplying or dividing.

Polarized sunglasses are a must. They reduce reflection, allowing you to see into the water better. Draping a bath towel crosswise over your head and under your cap so it is flush with the front of your sunglasses will cut out all side light and help you see even better.

Light-colored clothing is important in open circumstances because you will be less noticeable against the sky background.

Once you are rigged, it simply is a matter of getting out and searching. Whether you use a big boat on salt water for sharks, a flat-bottom boat in estuaries for rays, a canoe in freshwater shallows for carp, wade the shallows, stand on a ladder in the reeds, walk the shoreline of a drainage ditch, sneak through the lily pads for frogs, or whatever....your bowfishing fun generally is limited only by the effort you want to put into it.

The mountain country in the West is always a majestic sight, especially to a flatlander.

20

And Then
There Are Dream Hunts

The "Dream Hunts." What are they? Stone sheep? Barren ground caribou? Yellowstone elk? Mexican whitetail? Eastern turkey? Arizona javelina? Wisconsin whitetail? Grizzly? Black bear?

The most expensive hunt you can afford? The biggest trophy you can find? The best hunt you can have hunting hard but not running yourself to exhaustion? A vacation in great country, with maybe a decent animal to hang on the wall?

There are more than 31 categories in the Pope and Young Club list. Three are doubles—typical and non-typical divisions for Coues deer, mule deer and whitetail deer—and two—polar bear and jaguar—do not have entries accepted at the moment. So we're talking 26 species of big game which can be candidates for someone's Dream Hunt list. Add turkey and make that 27 species.

We might as well add turkey, for the bird, especially the Eastern and Florida subspecies, are tremendous challenges to a bowhunter, and the other subspecies aren't slouches either. Then, if we add javelina, the gray ghost of the desert, we have 28. If you haven't hunted javelina with bow and arrow, you owe it to yourself to try it sometime. That animal is quite possibly the best species there is for bowhunting. It can be tough hunting, it can be easy hunting.

It is often said that if you have the money, you can get yourself

There's no denying that a trophy whitetail buck is an impressive animal.

Maybe hunting an animal a little out of the ordinary is your goal.

next to a trophy-class animal of every species except whitetail deer. That species has the least relationship to a sure thing, yet it is available almost everywhere. The guy who can barely afford a beer Friday night after work in many parts of the country has a better chance of taking a buster whitetail buck than does a hunter with annuities running out his ears.

So should whitetails top the Dream Hunt list?

That's about like asking whether blonde women are the prettiest and guys with mustaches are the handsomest. It is all in the eye of the beholder.

Do you want the Dream Hunt or, possibly, the Dream Species? Do you want a trophy-class animal or will a decent male of the species which is a good representative of that species satisfy you? Is your goal to hunt a certain part of North America, with the species not as important as the chance to see and hunt through that particular bit of geography?

Is a Dream Hunt an outfitted three-week sortie in the

wilderness or the tundra? Is it a trip you want to take with a hunting partner or a long-time burning inside that doesn't care whether anyone you know goes with, as long as you get to go?

If you're a bowhunter, there's a better than average chance that the last person you want to mess with is an outfitter. Bowhunting has a lot of the do-it-yourself challenge, and some of the species and some of the different geographical areas become steps on a stairway to a bowhunter's personal goals.

Is your Dream Hunt a physical challenge you put before yourself?

Are you able to spend more time than money in the planning and execution stages, or is it the reverse? Do you want the Dream Hunt to be a one-time venture, or are you willing to invest time to learn an exotic—exotic to your previous experiences, that is—area so you become expert over the following years as you return again and again to that same area?

How old are you? What is your physical condition? If partners are to be included, how old are they and what are their individual conditions? Does age and physical condition matter? (The last thing a middled-age guy usually wants is a kid half his age, be that kid hunting partner or guide, running over 16 mountains in three days' time.)

Relative to the above, how much physical discomfort are you willing to put up with? How plush and/or modern must your camp be? What will the weather be like when you will be on your hunt? Is there danger of being snowed in?

Basically, just exactly what is it that lights your fire? You have to know, if your Dream Hunt is to stand the best chance of becoming just that. There are enough Nightmare Hunts around to last a couple more eons.

You will decide what you want to do, then begin planning.

Which area is best? Check the Pope and Young records. Check various state records. Talk to *bowhunters* who have been after the species you plan to hunt; they can be your most reliable source of useful information. As you begin zeroing in, talk with biologists in the areas under consideration. Talk with more bowhunters about those specific areas.

Make copious notes.

Ask not only of the species and the areas, but of the hunting styles to be used. Be sure that bowhunters you talk with give you that information. Ridge runners and stump pounders are not going to communicate unless they get the ground rules established early.

For many bowhunters, pronghorn antelope gets the ol' heart pounding.

You can easily get hooked on bowhunting black bear, not to mention some fine eating and a nice rug.

What about the elevation? Are you subject to the ailment that strikes many people the first couple days they spend at a high altitude?

An important factor in bowhunting: Don't try to do too much, fill too many tags, in too little time. This is an easy pit to fall into. You've saved for an Alaskan adventure, so as long as you're going to be there three weeks you might as well buy all the species tags you think you can go after. About half that will prove to be plenty. This is identical to the situation which made our Mother, when we were kids, tell us that "Your eyes are bigger than you stomach." Yeah, but the food looked so good, and we aren't going to have that special stuff again for a long time.

Repeat — about half what you plan will be more practical. This is bowhunting, remember. Tag-filling usually takes longer, a lot longer.

If you are going on your own, get as many topographical maps of the area as you will need. Study them, have them in front of you when you talk on the phone with biologists and other bowhunters. (You can do a tremendous amount of long-distance scouting, via Ma Bell, and you need to do it. Eliminates a lot of frustration and heartbreak. On-site inspection may be fine in construction and hunting, but construction begins with blueprints and you work with maps.)

If you plan to go on an outfitted hunt, call the outfitter and ask him every question you can think of. Be prepared to read between the lines when he answers your questions. Call other bowhunters who hunt the way you hunt and ask them for the names of outfitters they liked.

Remember that, as a bowhunter, you probably are a fairly independent person. As a good bowhunter, you want and need to be flexible in your hunting efforts.

Will the outfitter allow you to retain a certain amount of flexibility in hunting efforts, if needed? Or is it what he says and that's it? I know a couple of guys who wanted to go with a mule deer outfitter but lost their interest in a hurry when the outfitter told them they would spend all 10 of their hunting days in treestands because moving around loused up the hunting. These guys were ardent stillhunters and stalkers, and they were good at it.

You have every right to be treated with respect as an individual, not as a source of income, but this doesn't always happen. You can't know in advance if you will get the proper consideration, but you can have a good idea if you talk with

An outfitted elk hunt on horseback is a very special experience for many bowhunters.

enough other hunters and can read between the lines well enough.

Stan Godfrey, a dedicated bowhunter, has been on several outfitted hunts. He says, "I'd look for a good attitude among the outfitter and his guides almost as quick as I'd look for good animals. This is your vacation, your money. You want to enjoy yourself. You want to be able to work with the outfitter and guide, and them to work with you—congenially. When management is that way, I've found it reflects all the way through the rest of the crew."

If you want to sleep until noon, it should be all right with the outfitter; if you want to hunt 17 hours a day, that too should be all right with the outfitter and the guide who will be with you.

Doesn't always work that way, but it should. Some outfitters are more intent on getting big trophies on their scoresheet so they can attract more clients than they are in serving well the clients they have. Some guides aren't really guides; they are all the warm bodies the outfitter could find who would work under the conditions and time spans necessary in outfitting situations.

The first "guide" I had on an elk hunt, in response to a question regarding certain plants and whether they were elk food, replied "I don't know. Far as I'm concerned, there are pines and them that aren't pines."

There are good and there are bad. The bad are remembered longest.

Be aware that you and other hunters may be on the same hunt but may not get the same considerations. The theory is that all hunters are equal, but those who are making the third, fourth, fifth or whatever trip with an outfitter will be more equal than you on your first trip, and the breaks will fall their way.

By the way, the word "tips" supposedly is an acronym for "to insure prompt service." Sometimes the tip precedes the service. And not just in restaurants.

Unless an outfitter has outfitted for bowhunters, and unless a guide has guided for bowhunters, they can be disasters. Even if they have worked with bowhunters, there is no guarantee they understand the special needs of bowhunting and bowhunters, or if they do understand them will make the effort to satisfy them. But they ought to.

No Dream Hunt can be a sure thing. All you can do is plan and research the event, then go and do all you can to make sure your part of it is as good as it can be. The operating rule should be first to be sure that you are a happy hunter, then to get an animal for you.

Bowhunters willing to spend the dollars necessary for an outfitted hunt generally have a fairly good idea of what their chances are, and have accepted the fact that a bow can keep their chances down. Plus, they often place much more value on the hunt, the experience, the search and the chase, than on the actual animal itself. You want the trophy, sure, but that isn't the only thing, and some great hunts have been had where no arrow was loosed...and some poor hunts have been had which resulted in a nice trophy but nothing else.

Index